Sense and Sensibility
in
Twentieth-Century
Writing

A Gathering in Memory
of William Van O'Connor

EDITED BY
Brom Weber

WITH A PREFACE BY
Harry T. Moore

SOUTHERN ILLINOIS UNIVERSITY PRESS
Carbondale and Edwardsville

FEFFER & SIMONS, INC.
London and Amsterdam

Copyright © 1970, by Southern Illinois University Press
All rights reserved
Printed in the United States of America
Designed by Andor Braun
ISBN 0–8093–0448–1
Library of Congress Catalog Card Number 75–112395

Contents

v

Preface

Brom Weber was a colleague and friend of William Van O'Connor at two different schools. They were fellow members of the English departments at the University of Minnesota and at the University of California, Davis, where Bill O'Connor died several years ago. Now, in his memory, we have this book which Brom Weber put together, a volume rather unusual of its kind in that it contains not only critical articles but also poetry and even a bit of fiction.

In his Introduction, Mr. Weber tells a good deal about William Van O'Connor, to which I can add only slightly. Mr. Weber gives a general picture of O'Connor's career, naming some of his principal books, and he also provides brief but telling reminiscences of the man, speaking of his forthrightness and truly saying that "he displayed not a wisp of personal meanness." In calling the present volume Sense and Sensibility in Twentieth-Century Writing, Mr. Weber draws upon the title of the book which first brought William Van O'Connor wide recognition as a critic, Sense and Sensibility in Modern Poetry (1948).

My own slight addition to Mr. Weber's biographical sketch and reminiscence is a brief series of memories recalling the summer of 1961, when Bill O'Connor and I taught together at Columbia University, from which he had received his doctor's degree fourteen years earlier. That extremely hot summer I was also teaching (at night) at the Washington Square College of New York University, and living in Greenwich Village. I used to arrive at Morningside Heights early in the morning and, stepping out of the subway, would almost invariably notice a kind of lilac color in the air. I captured this in some color photos taken from the window of my office, looking toward Low Library; various members of the English Department asked for copies of these pictures, and I recall giving a set to Bill O'Connor. We hadn't met before that summer, but had once or twice exchanged letters.

He and I often ate lunch together at the Faculty Club, and I recall that we once went down to Gramercy Park to a publisher's luncheon-party. I had of course noticed those characteristics which Brom Weber mentions, the forthrightness and the total lack of meanness. Bill O'Connor was for the most part what is known as the quiet type, yet what he had to say he could say very well, forcefully.

During that summer he kindly invited me to write a pamphlet on an American author for the Minnesota series which he then edited with Allen Tate and Robert Penn Warren (the invitation depending upon the approval of his fellow editors). Bill suggested that I take John Steinbeck, whom I'd written of with some enthusiasm in the 1930s. But I explained that I felt that Steinbeck hadn't worn very well, and that Bill had better get someone else who wouldn't be, at that point, almost totally negative. He sighed and said, "Nobody seems to want to write the thing on Steinbeck!" I suggested for myself another American author I consider far better than Steinbeck, and the project was approved; alas, however, I've been so deadline-ridden during these intervening years that I've never managed to do that little book, about which the Minnesota Press has from time to time made friendly inquiries; though now I surmise that these are about to end.

The year before our acquaintanceship at Columbia, Bill O'Connor had brought out a widely admired book of short stories, Campus on the River. He told me that he had been trying to place a novel, and I offered to show the manuscript to a publisher I know and respect. This publisher, on being approached, said he had liked Campus on the River, and he agreed to consider the novel. He rejected it with expressions of sorrow; he and his readers simply felt it wouldn't "go." I don't know what became of this book; it doesn't seem to have been published.

But we had the pleasure, in this Crosscurrents/Modern Critiques series, of bringing out two books by William Van O'Connor: The Grotesque: An American Genre (1962) and The New University Wits and the End of Modernism (1963). The first of these volumes was dedicated to Bill O'Connor's colleagues at the University of Liège, where he lectured as a Fulbright Fellow in 1953–54. He had created amiable relationships with them, and at the 1960 Congrès de la Fédération Internationale des Langues at Littératures Modernes, which convened at Liège, his former associates there spoke glowingly of him to all Americans attending the meetings. It is therefore a particular pleasure to find that one of the essays in this volume is by Albert Gérard of the University of Liège, who writes most interestingly about Thomas Mofolo's Chaka, a highly important novel in the world's black literature, one which has been translated into English and several European languages.

Similarly, it is good to find other former associates of William Van O'Connor in this book, including Robert B. Heilman (with a brilliant essay on two modern plays) and Robert Penn Warren (with one of his first-rate poems)—two men who knew the young O'Connor when he was an instructor at Louisiana just before America became involved in World War II.

But the whole book is at this high level; Brom Weber has an eagerness for people as well as for literature, and he has rounded up a fine collection of writers and writings for this volume. One of the authors is Philip Larkin, the British poet discussed in the first chapter of The New University Wits. Another contributor is Vivian de Sola Pinto, who taught so long at Nottingham; Bill O'Connor had him teaching at Davis in his later years; his "London" poems are notable contributions to this book. So is the lively chapter by Karl Shapiro (also now at Davis), from a forthcoming novel—but there isn't space to welcome all these fine contributors. Brom Weber says that no single book about William O'Connor could possibly "be large enough to encompass all those to whom he meant a great deal as friend and writer"; and though this volume had to be highly selective, "the resultant collection nevertheless has a character that exemplifies the general sense of O'Connor's vitality and scope." All readers of this book will certainly agree.

HARRY T. MOORE

Southern Illinois University
May 11, 1970

Introduction

I first met William Van O'Connor at the University of Minnesota in the mid-1950s. Bill had a book manuscript tucked under his arm and expressed pained surprise that it had been turned down by a publisher who apparently admired his work. I thought Bill's attitude a professional oddity; he was not only one of the most distinguished figures in the Minnesota English Department, but also the one whose writings appeared most regularly and widely in the country. Much later I learned that the publisher who had rejected the book—it was published by someone else afterward—had a genteel conception of his role; Bill, after all, had been writing about contemporary British writers whose backgrounds were dominantly provincial lower-middle and working-class.

I was active at that time in the Minnesota American Studies program and apparently that led Bill to query me about how seriously, and why, I took such an enterprise. This also seemed odd, for Bill had been the first editor of *American Quarterly*, devoted to the interdisciplinary study of American culture.

Interchanges of the latter sort normally generate obsessive feuds in the academic community or, at the very least, misunderstandings rich with emotional stress. There was much in our particular academic environment, as in many others, to push me in those directions. Nevertheless, partially because of boredom with the intrigue prevalent in bureaucratized organizations, but in greater part because Bill O'Connor was so forthright and displayed not a wisp of personal meanness, I trusted myself more than I did the memories and interests of mutual colleagues. I never found any reason to regret my independent attitude as I grew to know Bill more intimately.

When Bill left Minnesota in 1961 and moved to the Davis campus of the University of California as chairman of its English Department, he affected his new colleagues much as he had me earlier. They found him extraordinarily unpretentious and generous; eager to advance their personal and professional welfare as best he could; always ready to scrutinize their manuscripts and to offer praise and suggest improvements with notable goodwill. If he had an *idée fixe*, it was this: the active scholarly mind inevitably expresses itself in the act of language. One could hardly complain about that, however, especially when he tempered his zeal with humor and did not seek to exempt himself on the basis of administrative chores.

He died in September 1966 at the age of fifty-one, an unfinished book manuscript on Sir Ferdinando Gorges on his desk. This work marked Bill O'Connor's return to a historical period with which he had dealt in *The New Woman of the Renaissance* (1942) and in which he was engrossed again during his year (1965–66) as a Fulbright lecturer at the University of Hull in England. Indeed, although his critical reputation was established in the modern and contemporary fields with *Sense and Sensibility in Modern Poetry* (1948), he wrote frequently and knowledgeably about many writers of earlier centuries. The wide range of his scholarship and criticism is set forth in detail in Robert Phillips' *The Achievement of William Van O'Connor: A Checklist of Publications and an Appreciation*, published in 1969 by the George Arents Research Library of Syracuse University, in which the O'Connor Papers are now housed.

During his relatively short lifetime, as Phillips' checklist amply demonstrates, Bill O'Connor was a prolific writer and editor. He had been born in Syracuse, New York, on January 10, 1915, and was of Canadian and Irish ancestry. He earned a B.A. (1936) and M.A. (1937) at Syracuse University and a Ph.D. (1947) at Columbia University. In addition to World

War II service in the United States Army, he was a visiting professor at many universities (New York, Columbia, Puerto Rico, and Washington) and a Fulbright lecturer at the University of Liége in 1953–54. A practical critic rather than a formulator of new theories, he wrote pioneering studies of Wallace Stevens, William Faulkner, Ezra Pound, and other contemporaries which significantly influenced judgment of their works and careers. In most of his literary studies, O'Connor upheld the major tenets of New Criticism, with some of whose most vigorous exponents – Cleanth Brooks, Robert B. Heilman, and Robert Penn Warren – he had been associated at Louisiana State University in the 1940s. Nevertheless, as his *An Age of Criticism: 1900–1950* (1952) typically reveals, he was perceptively generous to critics whose values and methods he found questionable. Literature as well as man evoked an admirably catholic tolerance.

Like other important literary critics of his time such as Edmund Wilson, Yvor Winters, and Allen Tate, Bill O'Connor rounded out his concern with the quality of literature by practicing it as an art. Some of his poems, which first began appearing in the early 1940s in *Poetry, New Yorker,* and less widely known magazines, were collected in *High Meadow* (1964). His poetic moods were dominantly lyric or satiric; in a late, unpublished sequence on illness and death, he plumbed painful depths of self. Self-revelation and ironic description of human behavior, particularly that occurring in the academic community, were major elements in his short stories, a number of which were brought together in *Campus on the River* (1960). Although he also wrote novels and plays (*In the Cage*, dealing with Ezra Pound's imprisonment at Pisa, was produced in Minneapolis in 1961 and published in 1967), O'Connor finally regarded himself as a poet primarily and devoted himself to that genre increasingly, even to the point of a relative lack of interest in criticism.

The O'Connor Papers at Syracuse contain a voluminous file of letters written by some of the most influential critics and writers of the past few decades in the United States and abroad. When the idea of a volume honoring Bill O'Connor's memory was conceived, it became clear that no single book could be large enough to encompass all those to whom he had meant a great deal as friend and writer. Though this volume, therefore, necessarily presents only a selective segment of those who would have contributed to it, the resultant collection nevertheless has a character that exemplifies the general sense of O'Connor's vitality and scope.

As might be expected, judgments of literature and its creators bulk largest in the pages which follow. Accordingly, two essays which analyze the present state of literary criticism and speculate about its future open the book. Murray Krieger is the author of *The New Apologists for Poetry* (1956), *The Tragic Vision* (1960), and *A Window to Criticism* (1967); editor of *Northrop Frye in Modern Criticism* (1966); co-editor (with Eliseo Vivas) of *The Problems of Aesthetics* (1953); and director of the program in literary criticism at the University of California's Irvine campus. Earl Miner of the University of California's Los Angeles campus has written on eighteenth-century English literature (*Dryden's Poetry*, 1967) and Japanese literature (*The Japanese Tradition in British and American Literature*, 1958, and *An Introduction to Japanese Court Poetry*, 1968).

The second section is comprised of studies of individual works by the contemporary English novelist John Fowles, the lesser known African novelist Thomas Mofolo, the English dramatist Harold Pinter, and the German dramatist and novelist Max Frisch. Malcolm Bradbury is an Englishman who teaches American Studies at the University of East Anglia; he has written novels (*Eating People Is Wrong*, 1959, and *Stepping Westward*, 1965), criticism (*Evelyn Waugh*, 1964), poetry (*Two Poets* [Allen Rodway & Malcolm Bradbury], 1966) and edited *Forster* (1966). Albert Gérard of the University of Liége is a Belgian critic-scholar and the author of *L'Idée Romantique de la Poésie en Angleterre* (Paris, 1955), *English Romantic Poetry* (1968), and a forthcoming study of African literature. Robert B. Heilman, chairman of the English Department at the University of Washington, is the author of *This Great Stage* (1948), *Magic in the Web* (1956), and *Tragedy and Melodrama* (1968); editor of *Modern Short Stories* (1950); and coeditor (with Cleanth Brooks) of *Understanding Drama* (1945).

Four American literary figures are dealt with in the third section of this book: short-story writer Katherine Anne Porter, novelist F. Scott Fitzgerald, difficult-to-label Mark Twain, and poet Ezra Pound. Howard Baker has written fiction (*Orange Valley*, 1931), an criticism (*Induction to Tragedy*, 1939), and poetry (*Ode to the Sea and Other Poems*, 1966). Richard Foster, chairman of the English Department at Macalester College, is the author of *The New Romantics* (1962) and *Norman Mailer* (1966) and coeditor of *Modern Criticism: Theory and Practice* (1963). Lewis Leary's scrutiny of the spectrum of American literature has carried him from the eighteenth century (*That Rascal Freneau*, 1941) through the nineteenth century (*John Greenleaf Whittier*, 1961, and *A Casebook on Mark Twain's Wound*, 1962) into the twentieth (*Motive and Method in The Cantos of Ezra Pound*, 1954); he teaches American literature at the University of North Carolina. Walter Sutton, professor of English at Syracuse University, is the author of *The Western Book Trade* (1961) and *Modern American Criticism* (1963), editor of *Ezra Pound* (1963), and coeditor of *American Literature: Tradition and Innovation* (1969).

Poetry and fiction, unusual genres to be found in a volume honoring a university professor of English, belong organically in this miscellany. Philip Larkin, the English writer, is a poet (*The North Ship*, 1945; *The Less Deceived*, 1955; and *The Whitsun Weddings*, 1964) who has also written novels (*Jill*, 1946, and *A Girl in Winter*, 1947). The late Vivian de Sola Pinto, who died as this volume went to press, was professor emeritus of the University of Nottingham and one of England's most distinguished contemporary men-of-letters; his many works include poetry (*This Is My England*, 1941), criticism (*Crisis in English Poetry 1880–1940*, 1959), biography (*Enthusiast in Wit*, 1962), and scholarly editions (*The Complete Poems of D. H. Lawrence*, 1964, and *William Blake*, 1965). Karl Shapiro, who teaches at the Davis Campus of the University of California, is a poet (*Person, Place and Thing*, 1942; *Poems of a Jew*, 1958; *Selected Poems*, 1968), who has also written literary studies (*English Prosody and Modern Poetry*, 1947; *Beyond Criticism*, 1953;

and *To Abolish Children*, 1968) and edited *American Poetry* (1960); the fiction in this book is a chapter from a novel in progress. Leonard Unger, professor of English at the University of Minnesota, is the author of *The Man in the Name* (1956) and *T. S. Eliot: Moments and Patterns* (1967), editor of *T. S. Eliot: A Selected Critique* (1948), and coeditor (with William Van O'Connor) of *Poems for Study* (1949). Robert Penn Warren, American man-of-letters who teaches at Yale University, has written in many forms: poetry (*Selected Poems, 1923–1943*, 1944; *Brother to Dragons*, 1953; and *Incarnations*, 1968); novel (*Night Rider*, 1939; *All the King's Men*, 1946; *The Flood*, 1964); short story (*The Circus in the Attic*, 1947); social comment (*Who Speaks for the Negro?*, 1965); criticism (*Selected Essays*, 1958); and biography (*John Brown*, 1929). James Wright's poetry has been collected in *The Green Wall* (1957), *Saint Judas* (1959), *The Branch Will Not Break* (1963), and *Shall We Gather at the River* (1968); he is a member of the English Department at Hunter College.

I am indebted to Robert A. Wiggins and to Earl Miner for aid and advice in the preparation of this book.

I also wish to acknowledge the permission granted to use material from an earlier version of Murray Krieger's "The Continuing Need for Criticism" that appeared in *Concerning Poetry*, I, 1 (Spring 1968); permission to use the revised essay by Howard Baker, "The Upward Path: Notes on the Work of Katherine Anne Porter," originally published in *The Southern Review*, January (Winter) 1968, IV, 1 (new ser.), 1–19; permission to use Lewis Leary's "Mark Twain Among the Malefactors," a revision of "The Bankruptcy of Mark Twain" that appeared in *The Carrell*, 9, 1 (June 1968).

Robert Penn Warren's "Bad Year, Bad War: New Year's Card" is reprinted with permission from *The New York Review of Books*. Copyright © 1969 The New York Review.

Davis, California   BROM WEBER
December 15, 1969

Sense and Sensibility
in
Twentieth-Century Writing

The Continuing Need for Criticism [1]

MURRAY KRIEGER

In a recent talk delivered at the Modern Language Association meetings, Northrop Frye suggested—in citing some of the evils of plenty in contemporary scholarship—that the profession might well think about administering a contraceptive pill to inhibit production by its new Ph.D.'s. The continuing multiplication of essays and books, of journals and publishing houses, all in the interest of a mutual inflation—whether of reputation or rank and salary—would seem to require some sort of curb. A more Popean or Swiftean view might see the profession in danger of smothering in its own afterbirth, or excrement, if the two are not in this case one.

At such a time, and sharing such visions of a new *Dunciad,* how can I justify the plea for yet more criticism implied by my title? Surely I must find an especially compelling reason for calling more criticism into being, lest I be convicted of pandering to a prolixity that I have recognized and lamented. Indeed, it is time, and past time, for only good reasons to justify adding to the heap of pages either in print or—even worse in the case of journals—committed indefinitely to the outpourings of periodic print.

Obviously, I must be calling for a special sort of criticism, a different sort from what we have for the most part been getting of late. How would I restrict the sort of criticism I am calling for? In suggesting controls for it, I would urge two propositions—not altogether the converse of each other—to be emphasized equally, one by way of encouragement and one by way of warning:

There is a continuing need for criticism.

But there must always be a continuing criticism of that need.

Let me first emphasize the continuing need for the criticism of single poems, even now, when it has become so fashionable to deny it—often yawningly. Events of the last several decades should make the anticritical swing anything but surprising. Ever since the revolution in the academy that followed upon the New Criticism, the abundance of discrete critiques in our books, our journals, and our classrooms has prompted the wearied cry, "Enough—and too much." So convergent has been the focus on the discrete work that we must have expected, as an inevitable humanistic reaction, the impatient demand to have literature returned to the human matrix that fosters it and is in turn fed by it. As critical method, fed less and less from a source of theoretical justification, seemed more and more to feed on itself, it multiplied its increasingly mechanical operations and its consequently lifeless products. The living body of the poems it dealt with was made more and more into a corpse: the critic's role, no longer the humanistic one of renewing the vitality of our verbal heritage, was becoming the pseudo-scientific one of postmortem, dissection become autopsy.

There has, then, been the inevitable reaction against this sort of critical establishment by those determined in their own ways to restore life to literature, to reassert the critic as midwife instead of as coroner. Some would destroy criticism itself by opposing mediation: by seeing its mediating function and the mediating function of poetry as suspect, as precluding life, draining that life from an object left on the dissecting table. This attack on criticism as it is restricted to single works is an attack on the objective hopes and disinterested pretensions of the critical exercise. Under attack here is the detached critic—the critic as analyst and judge—the critic coolly operating a mediating (meddling) enterprise. Distance between the critic and the work is to be destroyed as that which replaces human response with dehumanized analysis: distance creates the space for analysis and, consequently, the claim to a would-be scientific objectivity. But the critic's destruction of space or distance can be accomplished only by his following the precedent of the poet, who must be seen as destroying the distance an "impersonal" theory of creation would impose between him and his work. If the critic (or, rather, anti-critic), thus dedicated to process rather than product, must deny the distance between the work and its author, then poetry too comes to be seen as the enemy of mediation, of the mediating nature of language. The poem is at war with discourse as mediator. The poem is that paradoxical discourse dedicated to denying its own nature. It is to transmit immediacy, obliterating its own presence, a presence that threatens to deaden immediacy by freezing its dynamic flow into a static object. Instead, the work melts into an instantaneous union of "unmediated vision," shared among work, author, and critic, an undemarcated flowing of the vision among the three. And the spectacular—even apocalyptic—breath of life returns to inspire, as it re-humanizes, our traffic with literature. Thus it is that the central and detached concern with the object as a self-defined structure comes to be rejected because of its flight from the human contact with the object, the human contact that not only comes before and after the object but becomes the object, by merging with it, giving it its life.

The attack on the mediating properties of poetic structure and of the critical language seeking to fix that structure has taken several forms. The so-called phenomenological critics here and in Europe, perhaps most extremely represented by Georges Poulet, blur the work into the author's consciousness and ours, substituting a pulsating "interior distance," as subjective as human time, for the flat contours of spatial form, searched out by conventionally "formalistic" critics. Poulet's conception of form as static and dead—as objective —makes his anti-formalism explicit. The disregard for the single work as a discrete whole, as well as the impatience with the critic who painstakingly fusses over such works, must follow—and normally does. The "human" and the "interior" must be made to prevail over the scientific and the fixedly exterior if the vitality of literature is to be ever renewed instead of once and for all stifled. The results of such studies are brilliant, spectacular, even at times persuasively luminous—but not finally very transferable. They superciliously bypass the function of criticism as an educating process. Poems about poems, they impress the imagination more than the understanding.

The visionary critic like Harold Bloom has an even more open disdain for the discrete critique. Behind his treatment of the individual author (all of whose works constitute a single corpus) is an all-unifying, monolithic, transcendent vision that absorbs all works and their authors to itself. The breath of meaning, emerging from the organic vitality that moves these visions and makes them one, can be received only as we merge work with author (as creative imagination), merge authors into a "visionary company," and merge all with the sublime vision. Again the objective, as impersonal, as distanced, is rejected in the romantic denial of space, the romantic explosion of distinctions.

Ihab Hassan looks toward another sort of neoromantic apocalypse, an unmediated breakthrough to body from which the Word is finally excluded. The flesh, then touched in its immediacy, can dispense with the falsely metaphorical illusion that claims the Word-become-flesh. And when the re-won bodily realities of our instincts can rush in, the middleman of art need not—nay, dare not—enter. The writers who celebrate this "dismemberment of Orpheus," Miller and Beckett and a host of younger novelists, create an anti-art, an anti-word, directed at the extinction of art, at total silence.[2]

Such, then, are some varieties of the recent emphasis on the anti-mediation that militates against criticism. The would-be objective critic, who wants to defend his art against such skepticism by meeting it head-on, must begin by agreeing about the paralyzing consequences of mediation. He too must be suspicious of discourse as a mere medium, that which by definition precludes immediacy and which by its action freezes all flow. But having shared the visionary critic's distrust of the medium, he must yet try to exempt poetry from its deadening powers. Having condemned mediation, he must yet save poetry. He can accomplish this only if he does not deny the poem as object, that is, only if he does not force an immediacy in the poem's relation to its creator by collapsing the poem into consciousness or vision. To make the poem a special object, one without the object's deadly there-ness, its spatial "fix," he must be prepared to ask, "When is a medium not just a medium? How can a medium be free of its pre-destined curse of mediation?" And he must be prepared to earn and to believe his answer: "When it can be the thing itself, holding the dynamism of flux in its coils." For the poem as discourse and thing is motion and is in motion. Yet it is motion in stillness, the stillness that is at once still moving and forever still.[3]

All these are theoretical problems steep and troublesome. As such they demand something beyond the unquestioning, blithe pursuit of discrete explication, the sort of explication that in its late days helped create and justified the antiobjective reaction which now demands that we take such theoretical troubles—or else abandon to the visionaries the maintaining of literature as a live art and act.

The theoretical task is easier when the opposition to criticism comes from those who would over-mediate, those whose impatience with the tentative delicacies of analysis leads to crude interposings. For the tentative delicacies of the critic are his responses to the uniqueness of his objects, his efforts to fit his discourse to ever new systems that defy his common measures. And it is this uniqueness—the critic's tribute to that unmediating medium, that space-eluding object—that the stubborn over-mediator cannot wait to pause over. We have seen that, even if the critic must resist yielding to the anti-mediator who bypasses all form for uninhibited subjectivity, he still must try to preserve the special life of his object by fighting for its immediacy, for the medium *malgré lui*. But the over-mediator is finally willing to freeze his object by spatializing its form, universalizing it by absorbing it into common formulas—models—broader than the work (or, in cases, broader than literature itself). This sense of the model is what is placed between the work and our private response, shaping both work and response to our awareness of that model. The deadening effect upon work and response is almost enough to send us, by way of reaction, to the dynamic vitality of the anti-mediator, except that we know of that danger too. But we know we must not surrender his sense of life to paint a frozen model.

When we sweep aside the recently fashionable language of structuralism with its models, we find the very instinct for universalizing the individual work that lay behind the pre-New Critical attitudes, whether social-historical or biographi-cal-psychological, which made the New Criticism necessary. The unregenerate over-mediator, who preferred to learn noth-ing from the contextualist revolution, sounds pretty much like those who preceded that revolution as he tries to adapt the work to extramural commonplaces. For example, the social concerns of Walter Sutton, which move him to keep the lines between literature and culture at once and contin-ually and broadly open, are not markedly different from the concerns which prompted Ransom, Tate, Brooks, and others to make their defense of poetry several decades back.[4] Against such arguments as Sutton's, based as they are on the failure to grasp the organismic assumptions, the New Critical defense is still valid, although there is now the need to deepen its theoretical basis and extend its theoretical conse-quences.

Other more subtle forms of over-mediation also threaten to preclude the criticism of the poem as a unique language system. They all have their attractiveness to the extent that we cherish the encyclopedist's pretentious hope of unifying our knowledge and our languages. But the cost to literature as authentic discourse is high. The structuralist, like a Lévi-Strauss or a Jakobson, runs the risk of letting the peculiarly literary slip away, when poetic structures, general linguistic structures, and anthropological structures come to be stud-ied, not only as being analogous, but even as homologous. Again the methodological issues may not finally be very different from those that brought the New Criticism into existence. Of course, there are structuralist efforts that would preserve the uniqueness of the poetic structure and resist the adaptation to generic models; but these would appear to abandon the distinctively structuralist ambition and would pose no real opposition or alternative to contextualism. Or there is Northrop Frye who, like the structuralist, works from a model literary universe; but the overpowering shadows cast by his many-faceted monolithic structure upon the little lonely work have by now often enough been lamented. The over-mediation often shrieks its impositions, even as it excites us with the monolithic set of forms that structures the common human imagination and its common human dream.

I believe, then, that the alternative critical attitudes that have followed upon the criticism which emphasized discrete analyses of poems and that have been taken up in part as a reaction against it, have not removed the need for such a criticism and have not overcome the arguments in support of this need. Whether the anti-contextualist proceeds from the desire to destroy the poem as a mediating object by seeing through it to the poet's immediacy, or from the desire to destroy the poem's immediacy by burdening it with universalizing mediations, he has not precluded the need to preserve the object as at once object *and* immediate.

But we have noted also the extent to which these responses have been generated by failures within the critical movement and by a flagging of its theoretical impulse to justify what it was doing. Its evangelical mission to save poetry dwindled into the Sunday sermon, moving routinely from text to text. It is this explication for explication's (and ingenuity's) sake that late defenders of criticism must not resort to, must move beyond. If Frye's totally absorptive system is seen as too universal, causing total deprivation to the singular, the critic of the discrete must resist the mere compilation of isolated perceptions as part of an endless bill of particulars. This critic must at last move back to the world from his internalized systems: what has turned inward must at last, and in a special way, open outward, the mutually reflecting mirrors (to borrow a metaphor I have used elsewhere) must be transformed to windows that capture a newly visioned reality. The "new word" that is the poem, still fully released from what the old words had been, yet returns to our common language to enrich it by renewing its powers of reference. And the critic must help, not only in defining that new word, but—perhaps more crucially, if less easily—in tracing its return to its culture and language, illuminating as it goes. If the critic stops with mere explication of the system, if he does not return it to its subtle function in the world of reference, its redefinitions of language and of vision; then he may be sure that his own role will be usurped by the impatient non-contextualist, who will open the language of the poem outward at once and without taking pains, who will make it serve the world of reference in a vulgar way that deprives poetry of those special powers which the critic of the discrete poem should be dedicated to serve and preserve. And he will deserve to be replaced.

It may very well be that, only by his taking the theoretical issues very seriously, can the critic prevent himself from succumbing to the myopia which his endlessly attractive objects induce in him. He is obliged, at considerable pain, to convert a terminal experience of a self-sufficient object into an instrumental occasion: he must ask "why?" and "to what end?" even as he accounts for the "finality" that asks no more. Tempting as it may be, he cannot indulge the practitioner's antitheoretical bias if he is to maintain the high hopes of the art he has chosen to defend from those who would dash them, grind them into grist for their mill.

Let me demonstrate some of these hopes by commenting briefly upon a quietly modest sonnet of Wyatt's. Its directness and simplicity should permit my remarks to be unencumbered by deep problems of explication. Indeed, so flatly unadorned is it that it deceived even Douglas Peterson into underestimating it seriously, despite his being a sympathetic champion of Wyatt's plainness.[5]

> Divers doth use as I have heard and know,
>   When that to change their ladies do begin,
>   To mourn and wail, and never for to lin,
>   Hoping thereby to pease their painful woe.
> And some there be, that when it chanceth so
>   That women change and hate where love hath been,
>   They call them false, and think with words to win
>   The hearts of them which otherwhere doth grow.

But as for me, though that by chance indeed
  Change hath outworn the favor that I had,
  I will not wail, lament, nor yet be sad;
Nor call her false that falsely did me feed;
  But let it pass and think it is of kind,
  That often change doth please a woman's mind.[6]

What is at once apparent is the straightforward reasonability of the speaker. His calm and sensible patience is evident in his syntax from the start—from the line-and-a-half interruption that splits the idiomatic "use . . . To" construction. It is evident also in the metrical regularity (so rare for Wyatt!) which he seems almost to insist upon, whatever padding may be necessary. It is as if Wyatt, showing he can write proper rhymes and proper iambic pentameter when he wants to (or when he ought to), is emphasizing the all-passion-spent acceptance that produces the untroubled pattern, suggesting that his more uneven rhythms and imperfect rhymes elsewhere serve other moods. (Of course, our knowledge that this *is* Wyatt's work, as well as our awareness of his usual metrical irregularities, is central to our response.)

The speaker's reasoned acceptance is, of course, a dominant feature of the mature realism of the sonnet's anti-Petrarchan mode. The knowing calmness of tone is a match to the sad truths he, somewhat distantly, acknowledges. The truths he acknowledges are clearly universal, a common occurrence with men, as the "divers" assures us. How foolhardy and immature, then, is the Petrarchan lamentation, described in the first two quatrains as the common response of other men and rejected in lines 11–12, one line for each quatrain.

The unruffled surface of this painfully won peace, however, rests on an absurdity of its own, all the more shocking for its being so unquestioned: there is the single *unchanging* fact of women's *changing*. The fickleness, the caprice, the unpredictability, in the behavior of each is, when seen in the behavior of all, a general law; far from capricious, it is inevitable. Instead of wailing over woman's changeableness as an irrational or immoral response to kind treatment, the speaker simply sees her as a changing creature: he has an expectation of her changing almost as of a physiological

necessity ("When that to change their ladies do begin").
The unchanging fact of change, the persistence of change, is
pressed upon us with the repetition of the word. It occurs
four times, once in each quatrain, once in the couplet. Twice
there is also the curious juxtaposition with the cosmically
crucial, and yet maddening, doctrine of chance ("when it
chanceth so / That women change" and "by chance
indeed / Change hath outworn"). It is more than juxtaposition, though; it is almost an internal rhyme, just a shade
short of identity, "chance" and "change." So change, though
universal, is the product of chance, is one with chance. This
mutability sonnet does not, after all, proceed in accordance
with reason; in defiance of all that is reasonable, it proceeds
in accordance with caprice.

With this disregard of appropriate desert, with the cause-
less, chance-y shift from one strong feeling to its opposite
("and hate where love hath been"), it is no wonder that the
speaker has lost confidence in the firmness of words as
names. Not only does he slip from *chance* to *change*, almost
as interchangeable equivalents, but in consequence he recognized the instability of even as fixed a term as "false," leaving
himself unable to "call her false that falsely did me feed." Of
course, the poet is wittily assured that the entire sonnet
stands as his proclamation of her falseness, whatever his
disclaimer here. Yet the fact of chance-y change from hate to
love persuades him, despite his implicit proclamation of her
falseness, to dissociate himself from those uncomprehending
Petrarchans who call their ladies false (see line 7) and rather
to insist that this strange cosmology of anti-love must force
usual judgments and usual words to lose their meanings.
Thus, though she *has* fed him "falsely," he must not *call* her
"false." Instead he must see this acknowledged disparity
between fact and nominal judgment. For woman's *mind* is
answering to woman's *kind* (a superb rhyme). Hence he
arrives at her falseness, induced by change which is at the
mercy of chance (although chance universally produces the
same sort of change, so that chance and its change may be
erected into a cosmic law of the woman's world, the world of
anti-love). In acting falsely to him, she is being true to her

kind, with her kind defined by the absurd and amoral general law ("But let it pass and think it is of kind, / That often change doth please a woman's mind").

So the price of his non-Petrarchan acceptance is his reduction of women to the less-than-moral. From his own superior, human, moral position of rational understanding—of a constancy and a sense of desert that allow like to respond to like —the speaker condescends to these absurd, senseless creatures in their predictably capricious behavior. Far from joining the Petrarchan in placing the lady on a pedestal as an object of his worship, he has placed her well below man as a subhuman, submoral creature.

If we can break free of the tight context of this poem, we can use it to enter or at least to reinforce the world of the delicate sonnet, "Whoso list to hunt, I know where is an hind," in which the relation between lover and mistress as one between wearied but faithful man and maddeningly evasive animal is all-controlling. Even more, this poem renews our vision of that remarkable—and remarkably complex —poem, "They flee from me." In that poem the gentle, tame, and meek collection of lady-pets have now turned wild, using their naked feet, that used to stalk in his chamber, to run away. The sense in which they are—to use the language of "Divers doth use"—feeding him falsely is heightened ironically by our awareness that they before took bread at his hand. How differently, "They flee from me" assures us, he as the kindly human keeper fed them! Now freely ranging, "Busily seeking with a continual change," they are serving him "kindly" in return. [Surely "Divers doth use" give us the right to note a crucial pun here: one sort of "kind"—the natural, submoral sort—becomes an ironic confession of the other—human, moral—sort of unkind. Through the pun on "kind," the natural kind (and unkindness) and the human kind (and kindness) are shown to be mutually exclusive even as they are ironically confounded.] How these poems, self-generated, break outward into each other, move toward an absurdist anti-cosmos of love's fortune! And this very notion, love's fortune, opens outward further, beyond Wyatt, toward Greville and Ralegh. It is the Greville, for example, of

"Away with these self-loving lads," with its perversely Calvinist doctrine of love's elect, momentarily and capriciously chosen and rejected:

> God Cupid's shaft, like destiny,
> Doth either good or ill decree.
> Desert is born out of his bow,
> Reward upon his feet doth go.
>> What fools are they that have not known
>> That Love likes no laws but his own?

Here is a theology of love, that fancy god of fickle fortune. This self-enclosed, sovereign, arbitrary microcosm reflects no soothing Neoplatonic macrocosm. It can turn more serious, even deadly, as it governs the closed, bleak world of Ralegh, ending in the "fortune's fold" of "Like truthless dreams" or the universal violence, the wayward reckoning, not only of "The Nymph's Reply," but of the magnificent "Nature, that washed her hands." All this helps us to create our vision of the dark Renaissance vision of the earthly—in its emptiness of divinity—and of the poetic role of skepticism.

Such are the ways in which, hopefully, a poem, by working in its self-enclosed ways, yet opens up for us in unpredictable ways the world of surrounding poems and of its culture's inner reality. Let us try one more, not altogether unrelated, since its movement springs from the poet's awareness of the absurdities of language in its normal uses. The speaker's explicit distrust of language as names, perhaps reminiscent of Wyatt's concern with falseness, love, and hate, yields a special sort of anti-nominal system in Sidney's *Astrophel and Stella* 35:

> What may words say, or what may words not say,
> Where truth itself must speak like flattery?
> Within what bounds can one his liking stay,
> Where nature doth with infinite agree?
>> What *Nestor's* counsel can my flames allay,
> Since Reason's self doth blow the coal in me?
> And ah what hope, that hope should once see day,
> Where *Cupid* is sworn page to Chastity?
> Honour is honour'd, that thou dost possess
>> Him as thy slave, and now long needy Fame
>> Doth even grow rich, naming my *Stella's* name.

Wit learns in thee perfection to express,
  Not thou by praise, but praise in thee is rais'd:
  It is a praise to praise, when thou art prais'd.

Here again is a series of collisions within language, again seemingly simple and direct, though in the end this statement is more extravagant and—in the Petrarchan sense—more pious. The sense of controlled reasonability governs a string of outrageously irrational compliments. From the confession of the incapacity of words in the opening line, the verbal paradoxes ensue. Each key word denies its own meaning, each abstraction obliterates itself by being itself in a way that identifies it with its opposite. The very possibility of language has been precluded by the reason-defying perfection of Stella. Yet it is reason itself that justifies the impossibility ("What *Nestor's* counsel can my flames allay, / Since Reason's self doth blow the coal in me?"). The infinite reach of nature deserves a desire sanctioned by Reason itself. What a turnabout of the more usual notion attributed by Shakespeare's Adonis to the lowly desires of Venus, whose "reason is the bawd to lust's abuse"!

This is, then, the Petrarchan sonnet to end all Petrarchan sonnets. Impelled by the need to utter unique praise with nothing at his hand but common words and conventional claims, the speaker manages the farthest possible compliment to her who teases him (and us all) out of thought. The unsubstantial nature of words even makes Sidney's usual pun on his lady's married name—elsewhere no more than a species of "false wit"—especially appropriate here. It serves as a master stroke, revealing the final bankruptcy of words in their usual naming function ("long needy Fame / Doth even grow rich, naming my Stella's name."). The couplet is his final gesture, with its too repetitive insistence on "praise" (a form of the word is used five times), as the poet triumphs over his rhyme-enforced need to raise praise. Here is the paradox in which personified praise, rather than Stella, is praised by the act of praising her, so that it is she who wins over praise their competition of mutual elevation, as one last time the personified abstraction is outdone (and undone!) by the fleshly reality of her presence. Her unique immediacy has negated language, but has become its own language—the language of *this* poem—that has transcended the emptiness of language that functions only as mediation.

Out of the mutual blockages of language, then, the poet has broken through to his own language, with meaning newly restored out of the accumulated verbalistic wreckage of conventional meanings. Having achieved his riches beyond "rich," honor beyond "honor," a praise beyond "praise," he has been responsive to his reason beyond "reason." He has, for this poem, arrived at the absolute, substantive language of poetry's and love's transformations through their mutual finality. In concert these two, poetry and love, act upon normal language as eschatology acts upon history, both ending and transcending it. We are on the threshold of the world of *The Phoenix and the Turtle.*

But surely here, as with the Wyatt sonnet, we have done more than explore intramural plays of meaning. Or, at least, if this is what we have done, we have managed to come out with more than the formal display of their configurations. Surely the Sidney sonnet opens our way to what reason and love have as their visionary possibilities in this Renaissance world, even as language's shabby limitations have—in a shrewd, hard-headed manner—to be revealed to open the way. Here is a transcendent "golden" vision so different from the "drab" vision of a degraded love's fickle fortune, the first we examined, that keeps sharply distinct the drag of earth and the draw of heaven. Sidney's (in this sonnet) is a world of limits defied as the other was a world of limits sadly but wisely embraced for what—in their limitations—they could offer. Here, in the second, language is struggled against and transcended as reason is transcended; there, in the first, language was also an incapacitating instrument, changing like love with chance, and finally succumbed to in its caprice. The poet's victory over it was won only by his human, manly realization of his moral superiority as he resigned himself to loss. But in Sidney's sonnet (though he wrote many of Wyatt's sort too) language—like the lady, also a part of this world—can become transformed into the more-than-worldly

(I almost said more-than-wordly): there can be a break-through, not, as in Wyatt, merely a breakdown. Through the Wyatt and the Sidney we thus have even a new awareness of Renaissance struggles between Platonic and Neoplatonic—dualistic and monistic—possibilities in the relations between the poles of earth and heaven. So these alternative possibilities, ways of making and seeing in poetry, are alternative possibilities of the felt immediacies of consciousness and vision, to which we can have access in no other comparable way. Is our sense of language, of vision, ever quite the same again? "What may words say, or what may words not say" indeed! And what many things must it clearly become and continually be the function of criticism—after listening shrewdly to the words—to say?

So the theoretical need grants considerable license to criticism, but maintains a wary eye that insists it retain an ambition—at once theoretical and practical—that is commensurate with the need. I return, then, to the two propositions with which I began: There should, for literary scholars even at this late date, be no question about the continuing need for criticism—and for the detailed criticism of single poems. But perhaps more easily overlooked is the equal, if in part opposing, need for continual and self-conscious criticism of the extent and nature of this need, as we search out what further purposes we may serve by serving it. As inheritors of criticism's sins of excess, we can no longer assume that just producing more of it is by itself a good thing. We can no longer argue for criticism without first establishing its indispensability on theoretical grounds. Now this, of course, may bring us to one sort of criticism rather than another—one would hope a more vital sort, one that would do more than reproduce the same, wearying, self-serving, explicative circle. And this would be to bring criticism beyond itself. Is there a more profound way to serve it and to celebrate it?

The Double Truth of Modern Poetic Criticism

Somehow, and probably soon, the age of dissociation—which is to say, the age that invented and developed the concept of dissociation—must end.—Frank Kermode, Romantic Image

As Kermode's tone reveals, it is very difficult to consider at all closely the historical mythology of "the age of dissociation" without feeling a degree of irritation. Many people obviously accept the idea that dissociation of sensibility set in three centuries ago and believe that our poets have the task of joining what no man should have sundered. Obviously, some faith is necessary to sustain a poet, but more and more people seem inclined to believe that a poet is not incapacitated by an ability to think, or a critic by knowledge of history. The real problem is, however, that a considerable body of fine poetry has been written on premises, or at least with forms of justification, demonstrably false.

By now, everybody knows that T. S. Eliot declared that the two "most powerful" poets of the seventeenth century, Milton and Dryden, did some things so well that the capacity to think and to feel simultaneously was lost. Dissociation of sensibility set in, and not perhaps until 1922 was anything very much done about it. Everybody knows [1] that Eliot later half-recanted his anti-Miltonism and modified his doctrine of dissociation. Moreover, anyone who knows more than Eliot's conventional wisdom understands that Dryden occupied his critical disquisitions more extensively than Donne. We have been told that Eliot was not original, that his famous phrase came from Remy de Gourmont, and that years before him Stopford Brooke had said that the Restoration saw the end "of a poetry in which emotion always accompanied thought." [2] To all this, one is very much inclined to remark that poets and critics are as much entitled as anyone else to the discovery that fire burns and that poets must have unu-

16

sual capacities for conveying experience (including thought and feeling as well as other matters). But one may doubt that these discoveries are very new, or that there has been much value in the argument that because this art is so difficult the true fire is to be explained by the phlogiston of association, or undissociation, of sensibility.

Some day a full history of this critical phlogiston will be written. When it is, the historian will be obliged to affirm that even while critics, and especially poet-critics, were giving the wrong explanations, the true fire of poetry burnt steadily and rose, at times, very luminously indeed. While awaiting the full history, we may consider the general outlines it will necessarily assume. It will involve three poets as bogeymen—Pope, Dryden, and Milton; it will entail a mythology of the time when the crime was committed—the latter half of the seventeenth century; and it will emphasize a prelapsarian period—the former half of the seventeenth century: "the Baroque era," "the Metaphysical poets," "the Shakespearean moment," "the Elizabethan period," etc. The notion is one which we owe, like so much else we think our own creation, to the last phase of the eighteenth century.

"Is Pope a poet?" Dr. Johnson asked with full sense that he was. The question implied that others were putting the matter in doubt. Pope has never lacked advocates, any more than Donne, because all critics do not take leave of their senses at the same time. But the word "artificial" had degenerated to mean falseness. Formerly it had carried praise for what art might make under inspiration, and it had been a faith of poets from Chaucer to Goldsmith. Now a free spontaneity was prized, and the poet was not a maker but a be-er. Pope was a maker and a villain. But people do not search out a culprit unless they think there has been a crime. The crime was that someone had done something to the world that made intractable the experience which poets hoped to express. Pope must have been all the more exasperating in that he could write so brilliantly (though of course artificially), when nowadays others, whose minds and feelings were so much better regulated, should have such a deuced time with a sonnet. It was only human to turn the immediate literary difficulty into an ontological problem: something had gone wrong in the world. To Blake, the villains were the philosophers and the scientists, the cold, calculating sceptics. "Mock on, mock on, Voltaire, Rousseau," he scornfully invited, complaining as well of Newton.[3] To Blake, the remedy was love. We must love one another or die.

To the next generation, the remedy was imagination, because with the Romantic poets the problem had once again turned up its literary side. The age of poems about the impossibility of writing poems had begun. Keats was probably the first to argue that there had been a fissure in total human response, a disunion or dissociation. The proof text in *Sleep and Poetry* is too long for quotation in its entirety, but the implications can be grasped at once.

> Yes, a schism
> Nurtured by foppery and barbarism,
> Made great Apollo blush for this his land. . . .
> Ill-fated, impious race!
> That blasphemed the bright Lyrist to his face,
> And did not know it,—no, they went about,
> Holding a poor, decrepid standard out
> Mark'd with most flimsy mottos, and in large
> The name of one Boileau! (ll. 181–83, 201–6)

The passage is no longer the commonplace it was in the last century, or we might be speaking today of schism instead of dissociation. But James Russell Lowell, probably the most neglected of nineteenth-century critics writing in English, did not miss the point. Quoting part of the passage, he says flatly, "Dryden was the author of that schism."[4] (As his borrowing of quotations from Lowell shows, Eliot knew the essay.) No longer Pope, now it is Dryden who is the guilty party. Unfortunately, or fortunately, Lowell found it impossible not to love Dryden (by compensation, he equally emotionally disliked Pope)—and for no reason that he could clearly explain without making Dryden's virtues seem faults. The fascination with Dryden was bequeathed to Arnold, Eliot, and Mark Van Doren. The paradox of a great poet whose virtues were intolerable and whose faults retained glory obviously required some resolution, and Arnold provided it in "The Study of Poetry." Dryden and Pope had "admirable talent," and Dryden "such energetic and genial power." Further, Dryden provided us with "the true English prose." And so Arnold had his solution: "Dryden and Pope are not classics of our poetry, they are classics of our prose." [5] Between Arnold and very recent times, it is true to say of most critics what H. J. C. Grierson said of Van Doren's *John Dryden*—that criticism of Dryden has "writ larger" Arnold's sentence.[6]

With T. S. Eliot, however, Keats, Lowell, and Arnold were brought up to date by the introduction of a new villain, Milton. This was in some sense a step forward, or backward, because in the last century Pope and Dryden were continually criticized for not being Milton. Milton (and Dryden) lacked the admirable sensibility of "Donne, Crashaw, Vaughan, Herbert and Lord Herbert, Marvell, King, [and] Cowley at his best." 1921 was a good year for Cowley, at his best. And what was Milton's sin? It was "a dazzling disregard of the soul." [7] Chaos had come again, newly christened order. In the confusion that followed, men of great pith arose and did battle over Milton. To a later generation, there is left a confused memory of a Dr. F. R. Waldock on the attack and a C. S. Williams on the defense. And there is the experience of having read Milton another half-dozen times, at first as if stealing fruit from a forbidden tree, but increasingly with the sense of taking from a tree of life. This reversal has been accompanied by a rehabilitation of Pope and, more lately, of Dryden. And we have come to feel that Donne is more valuable as a poet than as a cause, and as a man than as a symbol. But the situation for which the critical phlogiston was invented still remains.

That situation is one of dissatisfaction with the world and with one's place in it, dissatisfaction with loss, with the breakage, division, and sterilization of experience;

> And, as it were one voice, an agony
> Of lamentation, like a wind, that shrills
> All night in a waste land, where no one comes.[8]

Yes, Tennyson had discovered the wasteland over one hundred and thirty years ago. Truly, these matters are

> Fallings from us, vanishings
> Blank misgivings of a Creature
> Moving about in worlds not realised,

matters, as Wordsworth recognized,[9] that might be the beginnings of wisdom in Romantic perceptions. The problem lies in isolation: "in the sea of life enisled . . . We mortal millions live *alone*." "Surely," Arnold asks—with nearly every other poet this hundred and fifty years and more, "surely once . . . we were / Parts of a single continent!" Separation and division hurt us; we are stricken with "this strange disease of modern life, / With its sick hurry, its divided aims." What was the healthy premodern age to Arnold? It was of course the seventeenth century, when the Scholar Gypsy flitted about the Cumnor hills: "Thou hadst *one* aim, *one* business, *one* desire." [10] Thou hadst, in short, unity of being, no dissociation of sensibility. We face division, and we long for a lost unity. "A conviction that the world was now but a bundle of fragments possessed me without ceasing," said Yeats. "I thought that in man and race alike there is something called 'Unity of Being,'" or at least he hoped so.[11] How was the unity to be gained?

To-day I add to that first conviction, to that first desire for unity, this other conviction, long a mere opinion vaguely or intermittently apprehended: Nations, races, and individual men are unified by an image, or bundle of related images, symbolical or evocative of the state of mind, which is of all states of mind not impossible, the most difficult to that man, race, or nation; because only the greatest obstacle that can be contemplated without despair, rouses the will to full intensity.[12]

What we discover from Blake to Yeats is a conviction of a modern sickness dating from the latter half of the seventeenth century, a belief that the sickness stems primarily from a lack of unity (between men, of the workings of the imagination, of being, sensibility, etc.), and a hope that the unity might be restored by certain remedies. To Blake, they included primarily love; to the Romantics imagination (especially of a sensuous kind); to the Victorians love, effort, and the soul; to twentieth-century writers, the image, the symbol, or myth.[13] Truly, it is a problem of sense and sensibility, as William Van O'Connor put it, or of the Romantic image, in the phrase of Frank Kermode. Whatever definition we give, the proper description of these overriding concerns may be reduced to two elements, primitivism and a search for unifying forms.

Of the two kinds of primitivism usually distinguished, chronological and cultural, the former has unquestionably been the more significant in the past century and a half or more. Gothic or medieval preoccupations held sway in the last century, but both then and dominantly in our own century the Renaissance and the earlier seventeenth century have best held the literary headlines. Obviously such nostalgia reveals more about the sigher than what is sighed for. The first half of the seventeenth century produced writers who are indeed of high price. But their proper value is real rather than symbolic. Apart from all else, the nostalgia has produced false history. The line by Donne, "And new Philosophy calls all in doubt," which is usually taken out of context and misapplied, suggests, ironically, the very doubt and dissociation of sensibility that the "two most powerful poets" of the century did not know. Of course the phlogiston of false history may accompany the true poetic fire, as Virgil's Augustanism or Shakespeare's Tudor myth show very well. What concerns us at the moment is, however, an unhistorical reading of history, an uncritical criticism of major poets. It is a terrible irony that the neo-Romanticism of our century should have paraded a pseudo-Classicism at once anti-Classical and anti-Romantic (and anti-Victorian). The attack on Milton and Dryden, the mudslinging at all Romantic poets but Keats, and the puffing of Lawrence over Dickens and Tennyson—these are symptoms of bad taste and false judgment. If our best critics have been guilty of such error, the follies of our Dick Minims have been beyond enumeration.

Unquestionably the dominant motive of modern criticism has been that of a chronological primitivism, of a retreat from what has been thought the actual character of contemporary experience. Along with it there has also gone a lesser cultural primitivism. Lawrence's Mexico and the India of T. S. Eliot (if not of E. M. Forster) are symptomatic. Perhaps the Celtic enthusiasms of a Yeats are as much cultural as chronological in emphasis. But the most important cultural primitivism of writing in English during this century has centered on Japan. Jules de Goncourt asked for France:

The search after *reality* in literature, the resurrection of eighteenth-century art, the triumph of *Japonisme*—are not these the three great literary and artistic movements of the second one-half of the nineteenth century? [14]

We may think that the search after reality in literature has been fairly persistent over the ages. The other two "movements" are, respectively, species of chronological and cultural primitivism. In the latter instance, French painters and writers made a major discovery, or propounded a major article of faith—that Japan had a contemporaneous relevance to the West. The belief is fairly striking in view of the fact that none of the important figures could either speak or read the language. So for our writers. Take Pound:

I trust that the gentle reader is accustomed to take pleasure in "Whistler and the Japanese." Otherwise he had better stop reading my article until he has treated himself to some further draughts of education. [15]

Or Yeats:

The men who created this convention [attributed to Noh plays] were more like ourselves than were the Greeks and Romans, more like us even than Shakespeare and Corneille. Their emotion was self-conscious and reminiscent, always associating itself with pictures and poems. [16]

And yet neither Pound nor Yeats could have written three words of their sentences in Japanese.

The sensation aroused in those of us with some admiration for Pound and Yeats and for Japanese writers is akin to embarrassment. Such estimates are even more remarkable—because based on less real knowledge—than the worship of earlier seventeenth-century writers. But the instinct is the same, and both admirations lead, seemingly inevitably, to the prizing of a unity gained in the "image." As is well known, Pound discovered in Japanese hokku [17] a technique of super-position and imagistic unity ideal for shorter poems: "the one image poem is a form of super-position; that is to say it is one idea set on top of another." [18] But what of long poems?

I am often asked whether there can be a long imagiste or vorticist poem. The Japanese, who evolved the hokku, evolved also the Noh plays. In the best "Noh" the whole play may consist of one image. I mean it is gathered about one image. Its unity consists in one image, enforced by movement and music. I see nothing against a long vorticist poem.[19]

For Pound the immediate aim seems almost restricted to the technical unity of image rather than related to unity of being/sensibility. But as anyone knows who has read *The Cantos* or modern criticism, there lay behind the technical aim a desire to find means of unifying inchoate contemporary experience. Yeats made Pound's technical point and the larger one as well. He thought he saw in nō "a playing upon a single metaphor," and upon seeing Itō Michio dance a role in his first "Noh play," he said that only then "did I see him as the tragic image which has stirred my imagination." After all, "Europe is very old and has seen many arts run through the circle and has learned the fruit of every flower and known what this fruit sends up, and it is now time to copy the East and live deliberately." [20] The brief lyric, the long poem, the drama; Pound and Yeats; the Imagists, Conrad Aiken, Wallace Stevens, and John Gould Fletcher; our more recent advocates of "Zen and haiku"—all show interest in a Japanese image, and all (at least in ideal and part of the time) reflect an urge "to copy the East and live deliberately."

Rather than try to see Pope or Shelley plain, writers in this century have sought to see themselves in Donne and his followers, or even in Zeami Motokiyo or Matsuo Bashō. There is no reason to wish a bad press upon these very important writers. But one may in conscience regret that from Blake to the present such enthusiasms have been accompanied by hate and spite for certain writers, that there has been so appalling a misrepresentation of literary and intellectual history; and that enthusiasm for Japanese writers has not been accompanied by knowledge of the language in which they wrote. How one longs for Ben Jonson's learning and his engagement with the present, for Milton's learning and vision, for Dryden's learning and catholic love of literature. For that matter, we could do with some of the positive criticism by Ki no Tsurayuki, Fujiwara Shunzei, Zeami Motokiyo, and Matsuo Bashō.

"Yet count our gains," as Goldsmith says. The many disputes from Blake forward have kept our awareness alive that poetry is queen of the arts. Arnold and others have dared to say that it might even replace religion. Moreover, in arguing the contemporaneity with us of Donne (or Japanese writers), critics have led us to look more carefully at the poems they prize and have called forth some very useful studies and outstanding editions. It is no small thing to have recovered for the collective modern cultural consciousness the works of two or three generations of excellent poets. More than that, the attacks on Pope, Dryden, and Milton have led to closer study of their works and a better appreciation. Finally, whatever its application, critical method has advanced. When literary history comes to be written, and to be important, again, it will inevitably be at a higher level of critical sophistication. What is perhaps most surprising is that understanding of Japanese literature has been advanced in one or two details. Pound's insight into the frequent two-part structure of haiku was corroborated almost forty years later by Donald Keene in his *Japanese Literature* (London, 1953). More important still, the unity of image perceived in many nō plays by Pound and Yeats has actually been taken up in criticism by Japanese scholars, not as a wholesale descriptive formula, but as a possible means of distinguishing the superior plays of Zeami from those of his usually less gifted contemporaries.[21]

Such gains are very significant. And yet anyone interested in the actual historical topography of English thought and poetry cannot but be dismayed by the misrepresentations of it in the pronouncements of poet-critics from Blake to Eliot.

In his *Sense and Sensibility in Modern Poetry*, William Van O'Connor laid out the modern intellectual map of past and present with a clarity and sensitivity that has not been equalled. Re-reading the book, one is struck by the way in which historical sense and critical sensibility have so often been at odds in contemporary criticism. It cannot be said that our critics have been particularly successful in the divine role of laying low the hills and exalting the valleys. Milton cannot be made small by calling him so, nor can poets make themselves great by invoking Donne. It is an irony that, weary as Clio no doubt is with the commonplaces, giddy as she must have grown with repeated misrepresentations, she will need to record faithfully that the false modern history of poetry from 1590 forwards is also true history in the sense that the erroneous view was talked of as if true by generations of writers. The greatest poet writing in English in this century was capable of saying in "Fragments":

> Locke sank into a swoon;
> The Garden died;
> God took the spinning-jenny
> Out of his side.

Yeats's lines are well known. They are powerfully evocative, both in their own free power and as an expression of a modern myth. Yet not a single assertion in the poem is historically true; the "myth" may be "true" but the truth is falsehood. Must we then return to Pomponazzi and assert a "double truth" for criticism from Blake to Eliot? That it is verifiably false but emotionally true? The question is a very grave one to anybody who takes seriously poetry *and* history. Or should we simply add ironies of our own to the many of Yeats in his rehearsal of one of the most powerful recurrent images of the poetry of the last century, the sea? At least the title suits our purpose—"The Nineteenth Century and After":

> Though the great song return no more
> There's keen delight in what we have:
> The rattle of pebbles on the shore
> Under the receding wave.[22]

John Fowles's *The Magus*

MALCOLM BRADBURY

Immediately contemporary writing usually presents a difficult problem for literary critics—such a problem, in fact, that
many critics confess to reading no contemporary fiction or
poetry at all. The problem is, apparently, that one is too
bound up in the issues of one's age to appreciate the forces
that make for literary survival; hence the literature of one's
own period needs to be sifted by the purging wisdom of time
itself before the clutter of distracting environment falls away,
literary merit becomes evident, justice is done. This means
that the first sifting is usually done by the reviewers, a
suspect body of men from whom critics generally like to be
distinguished. Writers themselves, however, have no such
independence they can claim. They are in it, stuck there in
time, and must do the best they can; and less and less, as
critics become more part of the academic than the literary
scene, do they have the critic's help. Perhaps this in part
explains one of the oddities of the contemporary literary
scene—its absence of an aesthetic consensus, its heterodoxy
of style, its lack of a prime mythology about the kind of
gesture that literature should make. A. Alvarez has called our
time an age of No-Style, and one sees what he means. There
is a marked absence of social myths and even of grammati-
cal norms; inclusive and significant literary structures grow
harder than ever to create. Yet we still have complex uses for
literature, and one such use is the making of style—the
giving of shape to our experience and the gestures of our
consciousness which is always a primary function of literature and an essential part of its service to its time. I wish as
critics we could be more interested in such matters, for it is
here that the livingness of literature lies, and the changes of
texture, tonality and myth in writing are of obvious consequence for our lives.

A convenient instance here is the contemporary English novel, which has not, on the whole, had much positive attention from critics at all. The thinness of the debate has, I suspect, led to a disproportionately low impression of the actual quality of current English fiction, and to a general feeling that better work is being done in fiction in other countries like France or the United States, or else in other forms like the theatre. The judgment may be true, but the amount of attention given to the postwar English novel still seems disproportionately low. It seems fairly generally assumed that aesthetic debate, technical discussion, and large-scale stylistic gesture are primarily the preserve of French, German, and American novelists; and though various English novelists—like Christine Brooke-Rose, B. S. Johnson, Iris Murdoch and A. S. Byatt—have in different ways attempted to state an aesthetic position or sustain a debate, the English novel is generally regarded as devoted to workaday practice. It would be easy to conclude that the novel in England hasn't in fact altered very much over the last twenty years—though since it seems obvious that modernism has lapsed and become an historical phase, and that there has been a necessary artistic structuring going on in all quarters, this can hardly be true. What is more apparent is that what changes have occurred have happened without much abstract formal enquiry on the part either of practitioners or critics. On the whole the critics—a good deal of whose critical theory is still mounted on extrapolations from modernism—have tended to accept the view that the English novel has not been very serious. Indeed probably no other form has been so readily taken at its face value, at its literal and realistic level—a tendency that has perhaps derived from the denotative emphasis that many postwar writers have themselves put on their fiction. The statements of several novelists who, in the early fifties, asserted their anti-experimentalism and realism, and frankly stressed their devotion to day-to-day social reality, seem to have given the English novel a basically documentary association that it has had trouble in escaping from. The stress on the factuality of fiction seems to have been taken oddly straight by many of the critics, particularly those Americans who have been almost the only book-length analysts of postwar English novels. But critics who historically are willing to discuss "realism" as a species of aesthetic enterprise seem to have found little to say about this fiction, or else they have concentrated on its sociological aspects to the exclusion of most other things.

This emphasis is critically uneasy anyway, but it has become more so in the more recent climate of English fiction, which has gone through a marked period of shift: away from concern with specific cultural detail, from that fascination with new social postures and textures, which marked much of the fictional activity of the 1950s. It was inevitable that the postulated relations of men and men, and men and things, of that kind of fiction should constitute a kind of challenge for subsequent writers, and for the same writers in their later careers. Inevitably new alignments and new demands have emerged, and particularly they seem to have taken the form of recourse to a much more "imagined," mythical, and romance kind of novel, the sort of writing we can see in the work of Iris Murdoch, David Storey, or John Fowles, where the attempt to psychologize and mythicize modern experience has been conducted with an increasing force. Yet on the whole little of real interest has been said about such writings, and about the power of fictiveness with us; the critical record has not been kept.

The poor reception of John Fowles's *The Magus* in this country seems to me a good case in point; here is a fairly clear example of a book that, in a better critical climate, would surely have won a great deal of attention. It came out in 1966 and was well-received in the United States; but it wasn't very strongly noticed in England itself, despite the fact that it is obviously an ambitious novel—if only because it runs to 617 pages and amongst other things rather evidently attempts a kind of psychic history of the West in our century. It is also a spectacularly inventive book—not nakedly experimental, but imaginatively bold and also imaginatively self-analytical. It seems, in fact, that sort of book a novelist might write in order to assert, for himself and for others, a sense of the possibilities that fiction might have if it wishes to break through its contemporary philosophical or aesthetic impasses. It also seems to be a book about the status that fictiveness and myth now have with us, and in its own terms an imaginative structure for dealing with these themes. In this sense it faces, I think, the problem of structure in modern fiction—a problem which seems to me to engross a good many important writers nowadays. We live in an environment in which it is hard for a writer to establish the literal reality of plot and character as a coherent meaning, and to express a fiction as a coherent linear development of knowledge. So, even as we intuit large and meaningful orders behind our experience, language and structure have become quizzical properties, not easily to be sustained by an appeal to a natural order in reality or to a positive and developing meaning in history. The problems of presenting the structure of a novel as somehow coequal with life become intensified and obscured when there are, in fact, no communal myths; the novelist is hard put to it to order life's contingencies significantly, even where he feels that there are orders to be appealed to; he thus feels a growing need to present fictions as fictive. He may do this by manifesting the oddity and unreality of his own role as narrator; or he may delegate the function by creating, within his fiction, the figure of a substitute artist who raises the problem. A number of modern fictions therefore have turned to the strategy of ambiguous revelation; there is within them a substitute author-figure who is both powerful and deceptive, the bearer of some suprarational wisdom who holds his wisdom in quizzical status. The psychopomp figures of Iris Murdoch's early novels—Hugo Belfounder, Mischa Fox, Honor Klein—who speak for an ambiguous philosophical or anthropological wisdom seem very much of this kind. They are the voice of forces beyond and outside the familiar orders of society and its states of mind; but they possess ambiguous myths which have a species of falsehood as well as truth within them. And this seems to me the essential premise of *The Magus*; it is a novel of psycho-history, but a novel which at the same time questions the status that myth has with us, and therefore explores the trick that fiction always is, the element of the charlatan that exists in the novelist's own role. To some extent, then, it is concerned with the familiar obsessions of modernism—with the hope that beyond the ordinary, contingent, and disillusioned world of real life there lies a meaning of fullness, balance, and regard for mystery, and the suspicion that this transcendent hope is one beyond life and time and therefore can only be a translucent, literary image. But it is also very much aware of the philosophical limitations even of the hope of redemption through an aesthetic unity; and Fowles does manage to create the sense that his structures and obsessions are not borrowed properties but fulfil a logical need to consider how the imagination now may design, shape, and give meaning to the world.

The Magus begins in a world of familiar day-to-day reality; it shifts into a universe of theatrical mysteries; and it finally returns us to the day-to-day world conscious that the mysteries are not simply a theatrical extravaganza but a species of vision about our own needs and desires. Fowles does this by creating around his central character and first-person narrator, Nicholas Urfe, a vast and complicated psychodrama enacted, at great and improbable expense, for his benefit. Urfe is a young man recently down from Oxford; and Fowles goes some way toward making him a representative figure for his age and generation, by generalizing about his psychic type and giving a social dimension to his feelings of disaffiliation, anguish, and despair. Urfe is a rationalist, an agnostic, and a hedonist, though he also possesses poetic ambitions and a strong feeling of "inauthenticity." The action of the book starts in London, when Urfe, unsure what to do with his future, meets and begins living with an Australian girl named Alison. She is emotionally more positive than he, but is herself uncertain and desperate and possessed of the same sort of death-feeling as Urfe. Then Nicholas gets a job through the British Council; it is the post of schoolmaster on a Greek island named Phraxos, and Urfe sees this in a familiar phil-Hellenic way as a possible route to a fuller life. When it comes time for him to go, it becomes clear that

Alison has fallen in love with him. Nicholas really doesn't want the entanglement and is indeed incapable of adjusting to it; he goes off to Greece with vague feelings of having won an emotional victory over Alison. But once he gets there and begins his job, these feelings shift into sensations of isolated despair, deeper convictions of inauthenticity, and an increased knowledge of the deathly element within him. The test of all this comes when these sensations—accelerated by venereal disease caught in an Athens brothel, a knowledge of the inadequacy of his poetry, and his general feeling of being marooned in an utter non-creativity—bring him to the brink of suicide. But he stops at the brink, insufficiently "authentic" even for self-murder, and resigns himself to a condition of *mauvaise foi*.

But now another kind of action starts up in the novel. Right after this, Nicholas comes across a villa in another part of the island and meets his Prospero figure—Maurice Conchis, its owner, who has already been threaded into the story in a vague and mysterious role. He is reputed to be an ex-collaborator with the Germans; he has some strange influence with the school; and Urfe has received a veiled warning about him even before he left London, from one of his predecessors in his teaching post. At his villa, Conchis is surrounded by magnificent, if sometimes obscene, *objets d'art*; he has the air of possessing a pleasured and privileged view of the world; and his life seems vaguely to contain meanings somehow related to Nicholas's fortunes. On invitation, Urfe starts to spend most of his weekends at the villa, half drawn into this mysterious and pleasurable world, and half wanting to expose it or at least subject it to rational analysis. Gradually the mysteries he encounters there take on a sequential form; they become a vast and continuing drama. First Conchis introduces Urfe to pamphlets on science and witchcraft; he also begins telling stories about a number of episodes in his own life, which moves through some of the basic historical events of the century—its changes in style and thought, its two world wars. At the same time these events suddenly start to be mysteriously recreated around the villa, first at a distance from Nicholas, then, more and more,

around him, involving him and threatening him. A girl
called Lily, a figure from Conchis's past life supposedly dead
during the First World War, appears on the scene. Nicholas,
trying to penetrate rationalistically through to the truth
about these fantasies, starts to provide himself with an explanation—"Lily" is actually, as she reveals, an actress named
Julie. But now that the masques begin to interlock with real
life, they start involving Nicholas himself; what to begin
with was a spectacle now becomes a web around him.

Nicholas tries to break away from his involvement—he is
falling in love with Lily-Julie—by going off to Athens, where
he meets Alison again. But this is no solution; he rejects
Alison for Lily-Julie, and does so basically because of her role
as an Edwardian girl, for she lies somewhere beyond the
sexual directness of the "androgynous twentieth century
mind." When he gets back to the island again, he is much
more involved in the power of the mysteries and begins to
see a line through them; they are a kind of fable of the action
of the godless twentieth-century mind, and also provide a
field of symbols and insights that might indeed give it meaning. But by now Lily and her sister Rose, another of the
actresses, seem to be moving away from their mysterious
subjection to Conchis and into Nicholas's world of "reality,"
so becoming available to his desires. Letters to England
support their story that they are actresses; but then comes
another letter—containing newspaper stories telling of the
suicide of Alison. Shortly after this, Conchis reaches the
culmination of his own story—his experiences with the Germans on the island during the Second World War. The
Germans order him to kill three resistance fighters; if he does
not, he and eighty hostages from the island will be killed.
Conchis refuses, in a vision of freedom—a "modern" freedom which is "beyond morality but sprang out of the very
essence of things—that comprehended all, the freedom to do
all, and stood against only one thing—the prohibition not to
do all." This idea of freedom is ambiguously left, as a force
of transcendence and a power of destruction; it is placed in
the modern world and the history of Europe; it is the theme
of the fables that have gone before.

This seems to mark the end of the mysteries. The masques cease. The party appears to conclude. And Urfe claims Julie, whom he believes loves him. But the final movement of the story is concerned with the complete penetration of all that has gone before into Nicholas's own life and his "real" world. Just as Nicholas and Julie, together in a hotel on the island, are about to make love, the masque-makers return. Now Julie proves to be one of them still, leading Nicholas into the next stage of the psychic drama. Urfe is carried off as a prisoner to the Greek mainland and undergoes a mock-trial. The masque-makers have now emerged with disguises from myth and classical legend and cease to be figures from Conchis's personal history. Then in the course of the trial they take on new roles—they reveal themselves as social psychologists, participants in a vast experiment on Urfe, whose life they know in full detail and document in the language of neoscience. In a magnificent set-piece scene, Urfe is taunted with all his psychic weaknesses and portrayed by his tormentors as a characteristic and typically distorted personality type of the modern world—autoerotic, autopsychotic, repetitiously hostile, dependent on aggressive sexual relationships which end logically in the destruction of the female partner (Alison). A parodied withdrawal-therapy follows. Urfe is made to watch as Lily is shown to him in a pornographic film; then she makes love to a Negro in his presence. After all this, he is told by Conchis that he is now "elect"—he is an initiate into the cruelty of freedom.

But Urfe, though released, is hardly set free of the web that has been built up around him. After returning to Phraxos, where he is dismissed from his job, he goes to Athens—and there he sees Alison. The news of her death has been part of the plot, and Alison, he goes on to discover, is also mysteriously assimilated into the Conchis world. So are most of his friends and acquaintances, most of his life; no individual is reliably out in the world of unmanipulated reality, and no past event in his life is free from their intrusion. In the final scene of the book, Urfe, still resistant to being totally enmeshed in Conchis's web, is led back to Alison, who has been escaping him. The question still remains, is she still within the world of the plot, or is she free of it? And has it been a plot against him, or a plot *for* him—a plot to lead him to wisdom? The final pages are ambiguous; we do not know whether Urfe has been saved or damned by his experiences, whether the mysterious powers have withdrawn or remain in his life, whether he accepts Alison or ends the novel in renewed isolation. Above all we are left doubtful about whether the masques and mysteries, which have been given such fictional density as an experience, are a diabolic trap or a species of recovery and revelation.

The Magus is, of course, mythic novel or perhaps rather a romance, and generically this kind of fiction of the mysterious web has a long and honorable ancestry. Indeed, Fowles himself draws on a number of significant literary allusions. Conchis is Prospero, magician, psychopomp—the mysterious creator of mysteries, the symbolist of the world of the unseen, the agent of the supernatural, the psychic force that can lead us through to a new version of reality. But Fowles deals with him in an ambiguous way, though in a way not unfamiliar in much modern fiction. An obvious comparison can be made to Iris Murdoch, some of whose better novels— A *Severed Head, The Unicorn,* and so on—involve a mythic universe in which mystery suggests the problems of a lost order or structure not available in liberal-conventional notions of reality. Like Iris Murdoch, Fowles is clearly concerned not simply with mystery for its own sake, or the vague evocation of powers undreamt of in our philosophy, but with forces and structures that underlie our rational being, sociopsychic forces that are not readily registered in the fiction of documentary modes. In Iris Murdoch it is, I think, fairly evident that we are invited "out" of society in order to see the powers which underpin it, powers which presume new relationships and new risks with selfhood that must by necessity be explored. The problem of the mode is that it characteristically involves a high degree of fictional faking, and there is a strong temptation for the novelist to create a sense of mystery and special insight which is no more than a numinously dramatic satisfaction, to build up myth for its own sake. Fowles obviously piles on the suspense by making Urfe at times less aware of what has to be going on than he should be, and the elaborate forgeries and ruses employed by Conchis require a kind of good luck to sustain the illusion which Fowles as novelist always grants.

Fowles's way of working the story is to identify his reader with Urfe and so, to a considerable extent, to sustain his desire for a rational explanation, an unmasking of what Conchis calls his "godgame." Urfe belongs to the world of the real and ordinary, and he is a natural violator of myths; because he is cautious of being drawn into illusion the reader moves in with him when he does yield. In Urfe, then, Fowles catches many instincts, tones, obsessions, and above all ambiguities in our culture—its distrust of myth, its sense of the validity of the real and familiar world, its suspicion of revelation and authority, yet also its desire for metaphor, its wish to transcend the environment which gives only a literal meaning, its search for density of being. All these things in Urfe—together with his appreciation of the more spacious relationships of the past, his sense of the possibility of using a limited psychic type—make him available as a neophyte for the world for which Conchis stands. But that world itself is caught equally well and with a like density and ambiguity. Conchis is on the one hand the higher rationalist, who comprehends all that Urfe knows and is one jump ahead—he unmasks the desire to unmask, he historically or psychologically locates the sentiments and fears amid which Urfe lives and finally does so in a language he understands. His "godgame" is not only an exercise in timeless and traditional hermetic symbolism; it is also a masque and myth about contemporary history. He thus provides a structure for the comprehension of Urfe's world, though it is uncertain whether Urfe does or can accept it. His dark but ultimate wisdom—the wisdom of serene endurance, the wisdom of the archaic smile that holds experience complete and stands above it, and which is vouchsafed to Alison in the final scene —is enacted within the terms of modern experience. It has the prophetic pull of Honor Klein's dark wisdom in *A Sev-*

ered Head, and the same sense that it is a knowledge beyond the novel's capacity to register; only an image will do. The primary action is conducted in relation to a hero less far along life's path; and, as with *A Severed Head*, the rationalistic underpinning of day-to-day life, with its casual sexual relationships and its vague codes of personal relations, is left behind yet without our knowing clearly what is put in its place.

But Conchis is of course not only the wise magician but also the faker, the sleight-of-hand artist enabled by his wealth, his gift of persuasion and his mysterious authority to dominate and transform his environment. As Fowles's epigraph to the book suggests, the magus is both the mountebank and, in the world of Tarot symbolism, the magician who operates the cards. The duplicity of role is structural to the book, though of course it also leaves it in an insoluble ambiguity: can a trick which reveals so much and costs so much in goods and spirit really be only a trick? And what, apart from fictive purposes, would be its point? Fowles leaves the interpretation open. If Conchis could be destroyed by Urfe's rational search, he would be nothing; in fact, he always dominates Urfe's world of "reality" as well as the fantasy world which at first is all Urfe credits him with creating. But if he were the total mystic, his wisdom would have to be rare indeed; he would have to provide a total version of the modern world. What in fact he serves to do is to draw us toward transcendental images which lead us outside the world, yet create a sense that there is a density missing from the rational view of experience. It is evident, at the end—when it seems the watching eyes are withdrawn, the theatre in which Urfe has so long conducted his actions has disappeared, when he feels at once escape and loss of "their" interest—that Urfe is the man in the Platonic myth of the cave in a modern variant: the man who has seen the real and then returned to life. The powers that he has seen are not, however, only those of art in its sense of an observed theatrical drama; they are those of art seen as psychic revelation. The dilemma it concludes with—that of how the orders and symbols which transcend life but also reveal and order it can really be mingled with it—is the dilemma of the artist himself, and it is in this sense that the book is a self-conscious inquiry into its own structure.

So of course the real magus in the novel is the novelist himself. The creation of myth in our modern employment of language is itself a precarious exercise. We use language to explore contingent reality and not to create systematic and numinous orders. But the rationalistic use of language (here roughly associated with Urfe) implies no logic, no structural unity. For realism and rationalism, our basic ways of making discourse, are a-mythic species of description; it is in this sense that we live in an age of No-Style. Fowles's purpose in the novel is therefore to create a context of illusion and a language of illusion which has the capacity to go beyond theatrical play and display and actually create structural myths. This, by confronting and connecting the world of rationalism and the world of illusion, feeding the former into the latter and then withdrawing it in its incompleteness, he does. Urfe's dilemma is at the beginning of the book that of loss of structure, and this he knows; that part of him which is the poet, the lover, and the man seeking a meaningful history of his age, in order that he might have an identity and an authenticity, seeks and values the magus. And the magus, whatever his deceptions, provides precisely that—a structure for feeling, art, and history which makes possible not only a fantastic world beyond "reality" but art itself. In order to create this awareness, Fowles has in the book effectively to create another language or at least another order of notation. To do that, a large part of the action of the book has to act in a world of feigning, convention, stylization, which we historically associate with high art, art as play and display. At one point in the action, Conchis makes a comment about novels: they are, he says, artefacts that make inferior orders. Fowles feeds the literal events of his novel into the hands of the myth-makers he has created within it, and so is able to create a sense of an higher artefact. But this of course leads him into a consciousness of the fictiveness of the enterprise; and if on the one hand he is able to make the shift from illusory theatricals to a suggestion of a more binding structure for modern experience, he must also sustain the fictiveness of that structure. It is in accomplishing this delicate balance, I think, that the success of the book lies—whatever its local failures. In an age of no-style, this sort of painstaking yet finally questioned mythography is about as far as the novel can go; and this, I think, is the artistic encounter that must finally interest us in the book. It involves, that is, a real encounter between modern man and art, and does justice to the dilemmas of both. Fowles, then, not only registers the fictiveness of fiction, the spuriousness of structure, but also its inevitable claim and its psychic urgency, and he does this against modern history. In doing that, he shifts the resources of the current English novel in a significant way, and so manages to suggest that power fiction may still retain, in relation to its culture and its world, fresh and inquisitive new alignments of experience.

An African Tragedy of Hubris
Thomas Mofolo's *Chaka*

ALBERT GÉRARD

If Madagascar is left out of account, tiny Lesotho—known until 1966 as Basutoland, one of the three High Commission Territories in southern Africa—was the first subsaharan country to produce a sizable amount of vernacular creative writing in the first two decades of this century.[1] Of the five writers who then emerged after being brought up in the schools of the Société des Missions Evangéliques de Paris at Morija, the most important was Thomas Mofolo: he is responsible for a remarkable historical novel entitled *Chaka*, which may well be the first major African contribution to contemporary world literature.

Although he himself did not know it,[2] Thomas Mokopu Mofolo was born on December 22, 1876. After attending several of the mission schools, he obtained his teacher's certificate in 1898. He did not teach much, however, and was soon engaged as secretary and proofreader at the printing press and book depot which the French missionaries had set up at Morija as early as 1841. He was very much interested in the rich literary and historical lore of his nation. He was also a voracious reader, although feeding on the simple fare provided by the local mission library. He was conversant with the Sotho Bible, the printing of which had been completed in 1878; with Azariele M. Sekese's collection of proverbs, praise-poems, ad customs, *Mekhoa ea Ba-Sotho le Maele le Litšomo*, first printed in 1893; and with the Sotho translation of *Pilgrim's Progress*.[3] In English, the library featured such eminent Victorians as Rider Haggard and Marie Corelli.[4] Several of the missionaries, especially Edouard Jacottet and the then director of the press, the Rev. Alfred Casalis, advised him to try his hand. In 1906, the mission weekly, *Leselinyana la Lesotho* [The little light of Lesotho], which had appeared since the early sixties, began to serialize *Moeti oa bochabela* [The traveller to the East], the first novel in the Sotho language, which was hailed as "un ouvrage d'imagination absolument original." [5] A second novel was rejected by the press; the present whereabouts of the manuscript, if it still exists, are unknown. Then came *Pitseng*, which was also serialized before it was published in book form, in 1910. Meanwhile, however, Mofolo had been cycling through the Zulu country in Natal, gathering information about the customs and history of the Zulu nation. This material he turned into his masterpiece, *Chaka* (1925).

Chaka [6] was a Zulu chieftain of the early nineteenth century. Before he was murdered by his half-brothers in 1828, he had built up the Zulu people into a strong nation, and he had carved for himself a large empire along the eastern coast of South Africa, where he had wrought havoc and destruction with uncommon ruthlessness and efficiency. Throughout southeast Africa, this period is known as "The Wars of Calamity"; it was remembered most vividly for many decades. The Sotho nation itself was welded as a response to Zulu imperialism out of the remnants of defeated tribes fleeing in the Drakensberg mountains. It is therefore not surprising that Mofolo, as an African and as a Musotho, should have been interested in the momentous career of that Zulu Napoleon. What is less expected, however, in view of the strictures legitimately leveled at the deficiencies of most modern African fiction both with regard to character depiction and plot organization, is that Mofolo's research and meditation and genius should have produced a work which is remarkable for the clarity of its structure, the sharpness of its psychological insight and the depth of its ethical approach. Although *Chaka* has been variously described as "an historical romance" [7] and "a Bantu epic," [8] it is really a tragedy, both in terms of construction and significance. It is a narrative tragedy in prose, built along the simple curve of growth and decline which defines the structure of classic tragedy at its best.

The illegitimate son of a petty chief, Senzagakona, and of a girl called Nandi, Chaka is from his very birth a reprobate in the eyes of the tribespeople, who want him "to be killed as being born of sin." [9] The word "sin" is both equivocal and anachronistic. In historical fact, the people's hostility to Chaka as a child had two reasons: Nandi belonged to the same clan as the mother of Senzagakona, so that the latter had obviously flouted the rules of exogamy; further, although Zulu society accepted premarital intercourse, self-indulgence pushed to pregnancy was considered a crime: "In those days in Kafirland, an unmarried girl who bore a child was put to death" (p. 6); it was only because the father was a chief and because "with the Black Races a chief is above the law" (p. 6), that Nandi and her child were spared. Daniel Kunene has put forward the view that "when Mofolo speaks of sin in this book, we know that he is speaking of sin in the Christian sense, and not of social sin in the context of the social milieu which constitutes the setting for his story." [10] It may also be that the novelist deliberately equivocates on the word "sin," using it, in this case, to denote an infraction of accepted standards, whether Christian or pre-Christian. This would be in line with the syncretic tendencies which characterize all of Mofolo's work.

When the chieftain's legitimate wives at last supply him with male offspring, he loses interest in Chaka and in his mother, who are left to their own devices in front of the increasingly overt hostility of the tribe. With great psychological acumen, Mofolo, in the first four chapters of the novel, goes to the very roots of his hero's fate. As Ezekiel Mphahlele rightly observed, "His career began as a compensatory response to people's despise of him which arose from the fact that he was a chief's illegitimate child. It was also a response to his brother's lust for his own blood and to his father's ill-treatment of his mother." [11] In clannish societies, estrangement from the group is the worst fate that can befall an individual. The numerous outlaw stories in the Icelandic sagas are cases in point. Chaka's suffering at being rejected by the tribe is the primary conditioning factor of his later development. His sense of alienation and frustration kindles an unquenchable thirst for revenge, which he will be able to gratify as a result of the bravery and resilience he has acquired in resisting the most cruel persecutions.

Chaka's boyhood comes to an end when he decides to seek redress at the court of his father's overlord, Dingiswayo, head of the AmaTetwa. On his way through the forest, "he reviewed all his life since his childhood, and he found that it was evil, terrifying, fearsome" (p. 42). The philosophy experience has taught him is that "on earth the wise man, the strong man, the man who is admired and respected is the man who knows how to wield his spear, who, when people try to hinder him, settles the matter with his club" (p. 42). This realization leads him to the ethic of unlimited self-assertion which accounts for all of his subsequent behavior. "He resolved that from that time on he would do as he liked: whether a man was guilty or not he would kill him if he wished, for that was the law of man. . . . Until now his purposes had been good. Henceforth he had only one purpose—to do as he liked, even if it was wrong, and to take the most complete vengeance that he alone could imagine" (p. 42). From a reluctant victim, Chaka deliberately turns himself into an unscrupled revenger. It is at that moment that he has his first meeting with a mysterious witch-doctor called Isanusi.

The status of this supernatural character in the novel was bound to raise considerable attention among the critics, not least because the beliefs of Africans are supposed to be just crude superstitions by a good many unenlightened people. The earliest review that has come to my attention was published in 1931 by a noted expert on the Swahili language and literature, and on Bantu folklore, Alice Werner; although it is very short, it shows considerable critical perception; Miss Werner finds that "the circumstances of Chaka's birth, his cruel treatment at the hands of his half-brothers . . . combined to set him on the downward path, so that we view him, not as an extra-human monster, but as a man with noble possibilities gone tragically wrong"; she thinks that Chaka's dealings with Isanusi in the novel "are due to Mofolo himself, and show an extraordinary degree of sympa-

thetic insight"; but on the whole, she considers that it was
the witch-doctor's "baneful influence" which "determined"
Chaka's career.[12]

The next brief study of *Chaka* was due to an African critic
who was also an intellectual leader of the Xhosa people, D.
D. T. Jabavu, who remarked that the book

> gives us a new impression of the redoubtable Tshaka in that
> instead of the hero of history who is rendered repulsive by his
> unbridled, unjustifiable and insatiable thirst for murder, we
> here get a human being we can sympathize with for falling
> through no fault of his, under the baneful influence of a
> sorcerer during his tender years that followed a miserable child-
> hood in which he was treated with heart-rending harshness. We
> sympathize with him in the same way as we sympathize with
> Shakespeare's Macbeth whose blind ambition is constantly
> goaded by his callous wife.[13]

Obviously, those early critics appraised the book against
the background of the traditional image of Chaka as a
bloodthirsty monster of motiveless malignity. They were
struck by the fact that Mofolo's interpretation seemed to
turn him not only into a human being with definable and
intelligible human motivation, but almost into a victim of
his malignant fate. Hence, presumably, their proclivity to
overemphasize the role of Isanusi and to load him with full
responsibility for Chaka's evil deeds. As late as 1947, we find
M. Leenhardt still claiming that "les magiciens exigent la
maturation du projet criminel." [14] But in 1948, Luc Decaunes, in what was at the time the best discussion of *Chaka*,
hardly mentioned this supernatural element, but analyzed
the book in terms of fate and freedom.

> Le rôle de la fatalité n'est pas preponderant. Le thème de la
> prédestination se marie ici curieusement à celui de la liberté.
> L'homme est libre de choisir son destin et c'est en toute con-
> naissance de cause que le heros entre dans le tragédie. . . . La
> volonté de puissance, chez Chaka, n'est pas une tendance innée.
> . . . Ce sont les persécutions et les injustices dont il est l'objet
> de la part des siens qui vont orienter son destin. Humilié, trahi,
> chassé de son village, renié par son pere, il n'a d'abord soif que
> de revanche, il ne souhaite que d'être détabli dans ses droits

naturels. Mais en réalité, sa condition de paria a développé en lui un véritable complexe d'infériorité. C'est ce complexe qui, mis à profit par l'esprit du mal, sera le ressort de l'action.[15]

In this mention of "l'esprit du mal," we still find the notion that Isanusi is a genuine supernatural being and a decisive causal agent in Chaka's career. Indeed, as late as 1963, Miss P.-D. Beuchat wrote that in the person of the witch-doctor "we are presented with a supernatural explanation for Chaka's succumbing to evil," because "at the most crucial moments, when subsidiary crises occur, the power is there to challenge Chaka's decisions and remind him of his previous undertakings." [16] And the Soviet critic, L. B. Saratovskaya, claimed that "Mofolo's book is permeated with the concept of fate, of a mysterious higher force which controls Chaka's actions." [17] Other recent commentators, however, have preferred to work along lines which had been suggested by Sir Henry Newbolt when he wrote that Isanusi is "the visible symbol of [Chaka's] own hardening ambition." The witch-doctor, said Ezekiel Mphahlele, "is a symbol of Chaka's other self," [18] and Claude Wauthier viewed him as a "personification of paganism." [19] More recently, Daniel Kunene has shrewdly noticed that "If we compare the thoughts of Chaka at the time he hears the wailing in the village while he is hiding in the forest, with Isanusi's words during his first meeting with Chaka, we see identical sentiments, almost identical words." [20]

It is as irrelevant to ask whether Mofolo actually conceived of Isanusi as a real supernatural being within the *Chaka*-world as it is to discuss whether Shakespeare believed in witches. The point is that the Sotho sorcerer fulfills exactly the same function as do the witches in *Macbeth*: he helps crystallize the hero's impulses, he coaxes him into awareness of his own desires and of their implications. When Isanusi, speaking of Chaka's ancestor, says, "If thou dost not spill blood he will take no pleasure in thee" (p. 54), he simply confirms the philosophy of status through strength to which the young man had come unaided during his earlier meditation. And when the sorcerer adds, "The medicine with which I inoculated thee is a medicine of blood. If thou dost not spill much blood it will turn its potency against thee and compass thy death. Thy work is to kill without mercy, fashioning thyself a road to thy glorious chieftainship"—he merely makes Chaka fully conscious of the logic and of the dangers inherent in the course he has decided to take.

At that point, we must observe, Isanusi talks in the assumption that the young man merely wants to be reinstalled into his birthright as the eldest son and successor of Senzagakona. Chaka's ambition so far has nothing that could be called illegitimate. It is Chaka himself who makes Isanusi understand that his aspirations are of wider scope: "I see," Isanusi concludes, "thou dost not desire the chieftainship alone; thou longest for fame also stretching to the ends of the earth, such fame that when thy deeds are spoken of they will sound like fables. This fame thou dost crave for as for the chieftainship itself" (p. 55). To which Chaka lucidly and candidly replies: "Yea, fame is sweet. I would not be content if I were a great chief but without fame. And the fame I seek is fame in war, where spears are wielded, and big men with thick necks and mighty warriors perish. I desire that I myself may win my chieftainship [i.e., not merely inherit it] that my fame may grow the more" (p. 55). This statement contains the seed of Chaka's political greatness and moral decay, but it will not germinate until much later.

At Dingiswayo's court, Chaka's story branches off into three narrative trends: his bravery against the chief's enemy, Zwide, earns him the honor of being placed at the head of Dingiswayo's army; he falls in love with the king's sister, Noliwe, who loves him too; at the death of Senzagakona (which actually occurred in 1816), Chaka is made chief in his father's stead, much to the fury of his half-brothers. In each case, his success is facilitated by the intervention of Isanusi's mysterious delegates, Malunga, who represents bravery and strength, and Ndlebe, who represents intelligence and cunning. Thus far, however, Chaka's overt purposes have been legitimate. Nor has any actual evil been involved in their materialization, devious and uncommon though the devices of Isanusi's envoys may be.

But Chaka does not hold himself satisfied with the vindication to which he was justly entitled: "I still hunger, I still seek," he tells the witch-doctor at the grave of Senzagakona. "Let the cow continue to give milk, lord. I pray thee use all thy power and all thy wisdom that I may reach the goal whither thou art bringing me, and which thou in thy boundless wisdom alone dost know. As for the spear of which thou dost speak, it shall be red with blood on both blade and shaft" (p. 96). From then on, the forces of evil and deception begin to creep into the story by carefully graded steps. At first, Chaka himself does not participate in their work: when Dingiswayo dies (this was in 1817), Chaka is not aware that Isanusi's henchmen have made arrangements for the king to be conveniently killed so that the young chief can succeed him at the head of the AmaTetwa. In a sense, this is a climax in Chaka's career: although he has acquiesced in evil, he himself bears no actual guilt for the murderous treachery that has brought him to the throne.

The point of no return is reached when Isanusi reappears after Dingiswayo's death as he had reappeared at the grave of Senzagakona. He explains to Chaka that further progress in power entails a new dedication to evil: "In some respects it is a difficult matter to win the chieftainship thou dost desire, such a chieftainship that if a man were to leave the place where thou now art, in his youth, on foot, and go to the bounds of thy territory, he would be an old man before he returned. It is a difficult matter, for it is thou who must provide the right medicine, and not I" (pp. 121–22). This medicine, it soon turns out, is the blood of Noliwe, which must be mixed with the food of the warriors. And although Chaka is willing to sacrifice his beloved instantly, the witch-doctor insists that he wait for a period of nine months, "in which to confirm his decision so that he might not wish to turn back too late when the work had begun" (p. 124). The true nature of Chaka's longing is made clear when he changes the name of his tribe from AmaTetwa into Ama-Zulu (which means "People of Heaven"), "because I am great, I am even as this cloud that has thundered, that is irresistible. I, too, look upon the tribes and they tremble" — and Mofolo, for once intervenes in the story to comment:

"we . . . must wonder at the arrogance and ambition of this Kafir who could compare his greatness to that of the Gods" (p. 125), adding, a few pages further, "Then it was that he sacrificed his conscience for his chieftainship" (p. 129).

It is important to understand the peculiar significance with which the murder of Noliwe is endowed in the total symbolism of the work, for the character of the girl and everything that is connected with her seem to be of Mofolo's own invention.

Describing Chaka's reform of the army, Mofolo mentions that he forbade his soldiers to marry at the usual early age.

He said that the married man . . . thought of his wife and children, so that he ran away and disgraced himself. But the unmarried man fought to kill instead of being killed, and to conquer, so that he might enjoy the praises of the maidens. All the same, Chaka did not forbid them absolutely. He promised that the troop that surpassed the others in war would be released first from this bondage of celibacy, even if they had not remained long in that state; more, they would be given wives by the chief himself. (pp. 136–37)

And the writer adds the following, highly meaningful, generalization:

The reader must remember that above all else on earth the Black Races love to marry. Often in speaking of the good things of life people do not mention marriage, because *marriage is life*. Therefore we can understand well how hard the warriors of Chaka worked to gain this reward. To set his regiments an example, Chaka remained a bachelor till the end of his life (p. 137; italics mine).

Mofolo provides another reason for Chaka's rejection of marriage: Marriage, Isanusi had advised him, "is a hindrance to a chief, and brings dissension in his house" (p. 119). Indeed, it was sometimes the custom in Africa for a newly enthroned monarch to kill, or otherwise dispose of, all potential pretenders. Chaka's bachelorhood and his enforcement of celibacy on his warriors, are part of a pattern which culminates in the murder of Noliwe, and which signals the victory of the values of war and death symbolized by Isanusi over the values of love and life.

Most preindustrial societies are plagued with high infant mortality; abundant human fertility is therefore essential to the perpetuation of the group. This societal requirement usually receives some supernatural sanction which appeals to the individual's sense of wider self-interest. In thirteenth-century Europe, it will be remembered, Jean de Meung had forcefully condemned the traditional Pauline asceticism of earlier official theology in the name of God's command that mankind should grow and multiply; this type of vindication of sex and procreation not only as a natural activity, but also as man's legitimate way of cooperating in the creative work of God, was later taken up by Chaucer in *The Parliament of Foules.* In many African cultures, a similar valuation of sex and procreation is operated through the widespread notion that a man's life after death can only be ensured and maintained through the cult rendered him by his progeny. Religious belief thus sanctions the collective biological requirements of the community in its struggle for self-preservation. Sterility, then, is a curse and a source of contempt and unbearable ridicule,[21] both because it makes a man or a woman completely useless to the survival of the group, and because it ensures his or her complete annihilation at death.

Self-imposed sterility,[22] as in the case of Chaka, is viewed as so unnatural an attitude in the African culture context, that it can only stir puzzlement and awe. But Mofolo turns it into an image of evil, the symbolism of which is clinched by the murder of Noliwe. As Chaka's beloved, as a woman, the instrument of human perpetuation, Noliwe is truly the embodiment of the forces of love and life in Chaka. His falling in love with her was the sign that, at that early stage in his evolution, he was still capable of redemption: it stood on a par with his devotion to Dingiswayo. On the level of Chaka's psychology, her murder illustrates his complete surrender to the evil impulses of self-assertion. In the wider symbolism of the work, it brings to its highest intensity the antinomy of fame and love, of power and life; it is the most repellent aspect of the overall destruction which is the only way to glory and might.

In his introduction to his French translation of the work,

the Rev. Victor Ellenberger writes that *Chaka* is "L'histoire d'une passion humaine, l'ambition, d'abord incontrôlée, puis incontrôlable, grandissant et se développant fatalement, comme attisée par une Némésis implacable, envahissant graduellement tout l'être, puis consumant tout devant elle, pour aboutir à la ruine de la personnalité morale et au châtiment inéluctable." This Nemesis, however, is no outward power: it is the very same immanent logic of crime and punishment which was at work in *Macbeth*. The murder of Noliwe marks the moment of Chaka's rupture with human nature, as does the murder of Banquo for Macbeth. From that point on, bloodshed becomes an addiction. The tyrant's downfall is linked to his rise by an inexorable chain of cause and effect. The growing extent of his power also increases the number of his enemies, and compels him to impose ever sterner control upon his warriors. He is therefore threatened from two sides: by those who resent his ruthless authority, and by those who want a larger share of its benefits, until his two half-brothers, from whom he had wrenched the chieftainship at the death of their father, pluck up enough courage to kill him. Historically, this took place on September 22, 1828.

It is obvious that Mofolo had fully assimilated the Christian view of man as a free agent, totally responsible for his acts. He makes a perfectly clear distinction, among Chaka's deeds, between those that are prompted by legitimate justice, and those that result from a fiendish lust for power. At every decisive point, the meaning and consequences of contemplated actions are fully described by Isanusi, and Chaka always makes up his mind in complete awareness of what he is doing. Few African works exhibit such a profoundly integrated sense of the meaning of freedom and guilt in Christian ethics.

Although missionary enterprise met with considerable opposition in Africa, there can be little doubt that the early educated elites, especially in southern Africa, embraced the gospel of love whole-heartedly. They soon realized that it did not exert any great influence on the actual behavior of the average white man. The Christian ideal of universal brotherhood, however, seemed to them palpably superior to the traditional ethics of tribal identity and communal hatred. But while the central idea of *Chaka* is coherently and impressively Christian, it would be an oversimplification to suggest that any other types of outlook were altogether foreign to Mofolo. Indeed, the last page of the novel is unobtrusively marked by the emergence of two other standards of valuation.

It is all too often forgotten that as a Musotho, Mofolo participated in the vivid legacy of bloody memories which his nation had inherited from the times of the Wars of Calamity; the Sotho people had suffered grievously as a result of Chaka's imperialism, and national feeling may well have played its part, side-by-side with Christian inspiration, in Mofolo's choice of this particular evil hero. Some satisfaction, one presumes, was involved in illustrating the workings of immanent justice, not only on Chaka, but also on the Zulu nation as a whole. Before dying, Chaka prophesies for the benefit of his half-brothers: "It is your hope that by killing me ye will become chiefs when I am dead. But ye are deluded; it will not be so, for Umlungu [the White Man] will come and it is he who will rule, and ye will be his bondmen" (p. 198). Writing those words, Mofolo may have felt some complacency at this reversal of fortune for the enemies of his people, particularly in view of the fact that Zulu resistance to white occupation had finally been put down in 1906.

But Mofolo was not only a Christian and a Musotho. He was also an African, whose native continent was being increasingly and irresistibly incorporated into the white man's sphere. Awareness of their African identity and of the need to overcome tribal definitions and differences was spreading fast among Bantu intellectuals in those early years of the century. Indeed, Walter Rubusana, who had edited the first anthology of Xhosa prose and poetry in 1906, Sol. T. Plaatje, who was to translate several of Shakespeare's plays into Tswana, and to write the first novel in English by a Bantu author, John L. Dube, who was to become the first Zulu writer of note in the thirties—these and others were at that time busy building up the South African Native National Congress, which came formally into being in January 1912. Owing to its privileged status as a British protectorate, Lesotho's active part in this movement was negligible. The feeling was there, however, and we catch a fugitive echo of it in the subdued pathos of the last paragraph of *Chaka*.

Even today the Mazulu remember how that they were men once, in the time of Chaka, and how the tribes in fear and trembling came to them for protection. And when they think of their lost empire the tears pour down their cheeks and they say: "Kingdoms wax and wane. Springs that once were mighty dry away" (p. 198).

It is difficult to escape the impression that at this final stage the Christian and the Musotho in Mofolo have made room for the African, who renounces for a brief while his tribal rancors and his new definitions of good and evil, to ponder on the past greatness of his race and on its present subjection, finding some undivulged hope, perhaps, in the notion that the white man's empire too, will wane some day.

It may have been this final impression which, in later times, was to enable Senegal's Léopold Sédar Senghor and Mali's Seydou Badian to extol Chaka, in poetry and on the stage, as the heroic, self-denying ruler, who does not hesitate to sacrifice the tenderest passion of the heart in order to ensure the greatness and to defend the freedom of his people. Mofolo's central conception of Chaka is entirely different, and, as far as can be ascertained, much closer to historical fact. The Sotho author is by no means blind to his hero's inherent greatness, but he judges him and indicts him in the name of an essentially ethical view of life. Apart from the technical skill and the depth of outlook which it evinces, Mofolo's novel is unique in its successful combination of traditional African and modern Christian elements.

Although *Chaka* was completed by early 1910, it was not printed until 1925. This delay is of capital importance for the literary history of Lesotho. First, in 1910, while the book was

under consideration at the mission press, Mofolo left his
country and seems to have lost all interest in writing; when
he was invited to the first African Authors' Conference held
in Florida (Transvaal) on October 15, 1936, he sent his
excuses; nor did he attend the second Conference, which was
convened at the University of the Witwatersrand, Johannesburg, on September 30, 1937; nothing came of the suggestion
—offered by several South African missionaries and linguists
devoted to the development of vernacular writing—that he
produce a life of Moshesh, the Sotho chief who had successfully resisted Chaka. Further, creative writing in the Sotho
language, which had made a promising start with *Moeti oa
bochabela* and *Pitseng*, with E. L. Segoete's *Monono Ke
monoli ke mouane* [Riches are like mist] (1910), and with
the collections of short stories composed by E. Motsamai
(*Mehlea ea malimo* [The days of the cannibals] 1912) and
by Z. D. Mangoaela (*Har'a libatana le linyamotsane* [Among
the animals, big and small] 1912), died out very suddenly; it
did not resume to any significant extent until the forties, and
then not at the Protestant Morija printing works, but at the
Catholic mission press in Mazenod.

The problem thus arises whether there is any connection
between the delay in the publication of *Chaka* and (*a*) the
complete silence which Mofolo later observed, and (*b*) the
general decline of creative writing in Lesotho. It will be
remembered that Mofolo had embarked on his literary career
upon the advice and encouragement of Alfred Casalis and
Edouard Jacottet. In 1906, Casalis left for France to take
care of his children's schooling. In 1910, Jacottet was en-
trusted with the responsibility of the printing press. In 1912,
the Société des Missions Evangéliques de Paris published the
Livre d'or de la mission du Lessouto. This contained a
chapter entitled "Les Bassoutos d'aujourd'hui" (pp.
441–512), written by H. Dieterlen and F. Kohler, three pages
of which (pp. 507–9) were devoted to a highly ambiguous,
not to say almost offensive, discussion of Mofolo and his
work. The novelist is introduced as "un homme qui n'a pas
eu de déception et qui, peut-être pour son malheur, est arrivé
à produire, pour ses débuts, une sorte de petit chef-d'oeuvre."

This "kind of little masterpiece" was *Moeti oa bochabela*. After a brief mention of his following two books, the authors of the chapter make allusion to *Chaka*: "Un quatrième manuscrit, consacré par le même auteur à décrire les moeurs des Zoulous, est en ce moment même entre les mains d'un missionnaire auquel Mofolo a demandé des critiques et des conseils." And they conclude: "Une telle prolificité est imprudente!" What, if anything, they may have thought of Balzac has not been recorded.

It is not unlikely that the man to whom Mofolo applied for criticism and advice was his protector Edouard Jacottet, and he may have been responsible for the appraisal of the book as a description of Zulu customs. While this is a stupendous distortion of its meaning and import, we must keep in mind that the French missionaries, although some of them were highly cultured men, were not literary scholars; and criticism before the New Criticism was usually impressionistic anyway. The novel being thus misinterpreted, it is not surprising that the missionaries should have been reluctant to print it. In fact, we ought rather to wonder how it happened that the book was printed at all.

According to Janheinz Jahn, it was printed in a garbled version, and this, Jahn seems to suggest, led to the resignation of Casalis.[23] Actually, Alfred Casalis had returned to Lesotho in 1920; he had resumed his various occupations, among others the management of the printing press. He tendered his resignation early in 1925: his age and health did not permit him to pursue his heavy tasks any longer; his departure was announced in *Leselinyana* of November 13, and he left in December. The first edition of *Chaka* came from the press in February, 1926. The records of the "Conférence des missionnaires du Lessouto" clearly show that Casalis was solely and entirely responsible for the publication of the book, which makes any tampering with the manuscript most unlikely.[24]

On April 21, 1926, one member of the "Conférence" forcefully deplored the printing of *Chaka*:

M. R. Ellenberger demande qui est responsable de la publication de ce livre, qui, à ses yeux, ne peut faire que du mal à ses lecteurs, car il est une apologie des superstitions paiennes. Il est étrange qu'une oeuvre religieuse comme notre Mission publie un tel livre; il ne faudrait pas que la valeur littéraire d'un ouvrage nous fît oublier les effets pernicieux qu'il peut avoir.

There is no mention in the record of any intervention in favor of *Chaka*; Casalis had left, Jacottet had died in 1920, and it may well be that the other members had not read it. The "conférence" therefore invited the Publications Committee to report on the problem. It added a recommendation which sounds like a warning to the new director of the press not to repeat the "errors" of Casalis:

La Conférence recommande au Directeur du Dépôt de ne rien publier sans accord préalable avec la Commission des Publications.

Presumably, Casalis had failed to request the agreement of that Committee.

One year later, on April 8, 1927, the report of the Publications Committee came before the Conference. The Committee was unanimously (although with one slight variant) in favor of the book:

Trois des membres de la Commission des Publications sont favorables à ce que ce livre soit écoulé, et même réimprimé; le quatrième demande l'adjonction d'une page d'explications, écrite par l'auteur.

The Conference accepted the advice of the Committee; it decided not to discontinue the sale of the book, and to reopen the discussion when and if the problem of reprinting it occurred. René Ellenberger, however, did not desist and expressed "la grande tristesse que lui cause cette decision, car il considère *Chaka* comme un livre mauvais, bien qu'admirable au point de vue littéraire." Clearly, he kept to the interpretation which had been defined some fifteen years earlier in the *Livre d'or*. There is some irony in the fact that it was his own brother, Victor Ellenberger, who provided the French translation of the book.

Whether there actually were new discussions before *Chaka* was reprinted in 1937, I do not know. The fact is that

it went through nine editions from 1926 to 1962, and that in
all some forty thousand copies were printed, making it undoubtedly the most popular best seller in the vernaculars of
southern Africa. It was also translated into English (1931),
French (1940), and German (1953).[25]

The printing history of *Chaka* illustrates the dilemma with
which both Bantu authors and Christian missionaries were
faced, and which weighed heavily on the emergence of written literature in Africa. An earlier example has been recently
revealed by Daniel P. Kunene:

In 1890, the then editor of *Leselinyana la Lesotho* brought an
abrupt end to a series of articles contributed by a reader named
Chere Monyoloza, concerning the art of divination among the
Basotho—the types and names of the different divining bones,
their various falls as the diviner throws them, the interpretation
of each fall to diagnose a patient or reveal some secret or fore-
tell the future, and the praises that accompanied each fall, etc.
Five installments were too much for the editor to take, and he
asked what in heaven's name was the use of all that!, an action
which provoked a mild protest from A. M. Sekese, a prolific
writer for the paper, especially on the history of the Basotho,
who argued that Monyoloza's interest in divination was purely
intellectual and did not mean that he believed in it. But Monyoloza had been silenced forever. And even when E. Jacottet, a
more broad-minded man, on taking over the editorship of the
newspaper, went out of his way to invite contributions on the
institutions, customs and ways of the Basotho, the whole thing
was a pathetic flop: The Basotho writers had learnt their lesson.[26]

Quite obviously, the missionary presses in Africa were
established, in Kunene's words, "primarily for the purpose of
bolstering up the Christian faith," and not for the purpose of
fostering imaginative literature. Throughout Black Africa,
the growth of a steadily increasing body of creative writing
should indeed be viewed, from a historical point of view, as a
mere by-product of missionary work. It would be rather
foolish to expect the missionaries to have rushed through
their own presses works which could be construed as trying
to celebrate and perpetuate so-called "heathen" practices and
beliefs, however high their literary quality might be. The

arguments of the Rev. René Ellenberger on this point were perfectly clear and *nuancé*, and, given his premises, legitimate. His error, and that of any others hostile to publication between 1910 and 1925, was in mistaking the book for an apology of pagan customs. Whereas the modern reader versed in the techniques of modern criticism cannot miss the ethical significance of the work, it is true that *Chaka* contains none of the overt propagandizing which Christian proselytizers usually seem to think is the most efficient way to spread God's message. Account should also be taken of the possiblility, or the likelihood, that the African readership might misread the work exactly in the same way as some of the missionaries did.[27] Actually, the fact that the manuscript was preserved for fifteen years and finally published, suggests that some amount of heart-searching must have been going on among the Morija missionaries. It is of course a saddening thought that their procrastination should have discouraged Thomas Mofolo from writing any more. Further, the inauspicious example of *Chaka* was probably an important contributive factor to the decline of creative writing in Sotho during and after World War I: it is a fact that the promising authors who had emerged between 1906 and 1912 henceforth kept away from imaginative fiction and either remained silent, or cautiously confined themselves to devotional writings. In fairness, however, it must be remembered that without the introduction of writing skill and of the printing press in Africa, Mofolo and his contemporaries would have remained inglorious Miltons, and *Chaka,* instead of becoming a permanent addition to the literary inheritance of mankind, would probably have been irretrievably lost, as so many masterpieces in the oral tradition of Africa are doomed to be.

Demonic Strategies
The Birthday Party and *The Firebugs*

ROBERT B. HEILMAN

Harold Pinter's *The Birthday Party* and Max Frisch's *The Firebugs* (both produced in 1958, though *The Firebugs* first existed as a radio play in 1953) may be thought of together because they have some remarkable similarities. In each play the action takes place in a private house (all in the living room, in the Pinter; two-thirds of it in the living room and the rest in the attic, in the Frisch), and mysterious visitors finish off an occupant. Granted, the Boles place in *The Birthday Party* is said to be a rooming house, and the victim is a roomer, while in *The Firebugs* the victim is the owner of the house. Yet in each play the main action is the violation of a sanctuary; the traditional place of safety becomes frighteningly vulnerable to tough, insinuating intruders, who in each play bring their insidious evil to a head at a party, with its superficial air of gaiety and spontaneity. Above all, each playwright introduces a pair of sinister invaders—Goldberg and McCann in *The Birthday Party,* and Schmitz and Eisenring in *The Firebugs.* Both pairs boldly push their way in, though the two victims, Stanley Webber in the Pinter, and Biedermann in the Frisch, make some ineffectual resistance; they have an effrontery which their victims cannot cope with. Their end is injury and destruction: Goldberg and McCann produce "nervous breakdowns" in their victims, Schmitz and Eisenring incinerate theirs. As outsiders who come in to disturb, subvert, or ruin, they bring to mind Hardy's "Mephistophelian visitants" in Wessex. In their strange power they seem demonic, and we are not surprised when, in an Epilogue, Frisch has Schmitz and Eisenring appear literally as devils in hell (one as a royal "Personage," the other as Beelzebub).

Though he does this in a somewhat jesting codicil, Frisch openly invites a mythic reading: throughout, our imaginations identify a representative, unlocalized fable rather than a topical documentary. Pinter gives Goldberg and McCann variable first names (Simey, Nat, Benny; Dermot, Shaemus), as if their identities were more than individual; McCann calls Stanley "Judas" and sings a song beginning "Oh, the Garden of Eden has vanished, they say" (act 2).[1] But it is less such hints than the continuing air of the cryptic and undefined, of wily and ruthless potency in Goldberg and McCann, that makes the realistic sense of character seem inadequate and leads us spontaneously to see in them the typal and generic cast of mythic beings. At the end they take Stanley away in a long black car. They might, many readers feel, be "taking him for a ride" or to a less spectacular funeral; but they are also like demons taking a lost soul off to hell, as at the end of *Dr. Faustus* or morality plays. In *The Firebugs* Schmitz and Eisenring put on a little parody of von Hofmannsthal's *Jedermann* in which they call Biedermann "Everymann" and Schmitz seems the "Angel of Death" (scene 8).[2] They are indeed death for Biedermann, and they take him off to hell. Insofar as these pairs, in their malice and power, seem demonic, we can think of both plays as reinterpreting an ancient myth of evil by identifying modern incarnations of the diabolic spirit and their victims.

On the other hand, with their small casts and their adherence to the "unities," *The Birthday Party* and *The Firebugs* might be family problem plays like Ibsen's. But while the theatrical location is domestic, the moral scene is societal. In representing society on the stage, the dramatist has a technical option that is of some interest. We might expect him, since society implies numbers, automatically to use a large cast. Yet a large cast does not compel a social focus. There are large casts in *Lear* and *Macbeth*, where the essential action is within private consciousness rather than in society; the societal phase of the action only mirrors or echoes the private. However, the full stage does betoken a social panorama in Arthur Miller's *Crucible* (1953), Friedrich Duerrenmatt's *The Visit* (1956), Eugene Ionesco's *The Rhinoceros* (1959), and Frisch's *Andorra* (1961). Dramatists use numbers when the effect depends on number and variety of responses to an issue, or an identity of response lying behind a variety of façades or clad in a variety of styles; on the interplay of sameness and difference; or on the spreading movement of infection or, more rarely, recovery. When they concentrate social reality into a few key figures, dramatists have another end in view—to stress the uniformity of spirit animating a society rather than the diversity of its manifestations.

Frisch shows that his scene is societal by naming his lead "Biedermann" or "honest fellow"; it suggests the ordinary citizen rather than the especially sentient being who undergoes an inner ordeal. The Chorus of Firemen, who call themselves "Guardians of the City" and who appear in six of the eight scenes, betoken the public action. The fire at Biedermann's is not unique; we are never allowed to forget that there has been an epidemic of arson in the town. Likewise in Pinter repetition clues us in on the societal nature of the action. While preparing to get to work on Stanley Webber, Goldberg and McCann talk about other "jobs" they have done, and Goldberg explains to McCann that while the new job is "singular," still "certain elements" of it may be familiar (act 1). When Stanley has a "nervous breakdown," Goldberg alludes to other crack-ups that have occurred (act 3). He notes that "sometimes they recover, in one way or another." The event that keeps happening is in the public domain or some phase of it; transactions among persons or groups recur, while a spiritual crisis, however representative, is unique. No line in a tragedy ever suggests that the hero's drama is one in a continuing series.

A play may be focused on a man, on man, or on men. When we look at a man, the natural form is tragedy; at man, philosophic drama; at men, the drama of society, with its older conflict between folly and good sense, or, as is more usual with us, its troubled course between illness and health. The distinction obviously runs the risk of being too pat, and we should say quickly that the forms overlap or run together. Nevertheless, the ideal types permit some relevant discriminations.

Shakespearean tragedies are focused on *a* man—on a Lear

or Hamlet. Other men may be well characterized, but they are significant only because they are in the orbit of the protagonist. Though we tend to see man in *a* man, that is, to impose a philosophic configuration upon the tragic hero, this is a secondary response, a way of trying to define a great personality; what primarily engages us is the extraordinary individual named Hamlet or Lear. But when the dramatist is philosophically oriented—when what engages his imagination is not so much human beings as such than a conception of or a theorem about humankind—the image that he gives us is that of man, of an essence which, though it is distilled into a moving and talking figure, seems abstracted or generalized rather than individual. For illustration we need only mention *Everyman*. Not that we lack morality plays in our own day. When Brecht's figures behave as they are evidently meant to do—they don't always, for in Brecht the artist is always trying to unfrock the social philosopher—they tend to be demonstrative, man arranged in one stance or another. In *The Good Woman of Setzuan* we do not easily remember individuals, but what is unforgettable is the image of human self-interest pervading the town. In Albee's *Tiny Alice* we remember the characters less as personalities than as embodiments of concepts which we are endeavoring to define. In Beckett's *Waiting for Godot* Didi and Gogo, and for that matter even Pozzo, are less set off from each other than drawn toward a common center where they stand for mankind; the drama is philosophical, and it plunges us immediately into questions of meaning such as we ask only at a later stage if initially we respond to strong, sharply distinguished personalities. Beckett is hardly ever interested in *a* man: his subject is man—in *Godot*, man in his eternal posture of expectation and disappointment, with its quixotic mixture of fatuity and nobility.

The dramatist of men, though he may portray sharply outlined individuals and stir us to speculative activity about man, looks primarily at the behavior of men in communities or societies. Here we come back to *The Birthday Party* and *The Firebugs*, which I have called dramas of society but which have small casts. Their subject is "men," but in for-

mat they have something of the drama of "man." They are
instinctively trying to do it both ways—to portray the world
of men but to imply that these men in a society, which is a
specific entity in time and place, are also mankind, dateless
and placeless. Frisch does it openly, as we have seen, by
calling Biedermann "Everyman" and identifying Schmitz
and Eisenring as devils; Pinter makes us seek out the human
generalities latent in Stanley, Goldberg, and McCann. The
generic fusion in these plays—of social drama and morality
play—widens out the theme to the utmost. Surely some of
the effectiveness—the sense of the sinister—is due to the fact
that the triumphs of a cocksure evil pair over a victim who
cannot resist effectually reflect an aggressiveness and a vulnerability that are not historical accidents but human con-
stants.

One more theoretical point: what I have called the
"drama of society"—as distinguished from tragedy and philosophic drama—varies with history: formally, it alters when it
alteration finds. We can distinguish three major manifestations of social drama. Traditionally men in their social aspect
are the materials of comedy. This remains true as long as it
can be felt—we see this, for the most part, in Ben Jonson,
Molière, Congreve, and even Sheridan—that society embod-
ies workable norms, those of "good sense" or "common
sense," which are the measure of private excesses and devia-
tions, of the idiosyncratic and anarchic. The idiomatic plot
of comedy is the benevolent maintenance or recovery of
authority by the rational order symbolized in society at its
best; yet it is a flexible authority that tolerates compromise
with individual sensibility. In the great Romantic shift of
values, however, the individual sensibility becomes the sole
repository of truth, and the social order suspect—as sterile,
rigid, and oppressive. In drama for the public stage, the big
turning point comes in Ibsen's middle period: in *Ghosts,
Pillars of Society,* and *An Enemy of the People* the perver-
sion or corruption is found in the social order itself. This
paves the way for numerous twentieth-century dramas that
present men in their societal existence as unsympathetic,
false, prejudiced, inflexible, and irrational. In the romantic

view of things, the villain is the "establishment," that is, all those who operate the indispensable machinery of order. They are declared villains by fiat, or become villains when, in the maintenance of order, they exercise a political, social, or psychological power that appears to exceed the requirements of order. They are called repressive, punitive, and tyrannical.

Though anti-establishmentarianism is anything but passé, its extreme manifestations herald, and have already led partly into, another phase of societal experience which certain dramatists have foreseen and which, unless we are lucky, we may still have to live through. In this phase, the social order becomes very weak or breaks down, and the individual runs rampant. Liberty expands into an overall libertinism; libertinism seems inevitably to be the façade of, or to release, destructiveness; this is committed to finishing off the "old order" permanently, often with no alternative in view. Ionesco's *Rhinoceros* dramatizes the failure of a wide range of current beliefs and codes to protect society against an epidemic of irrationalism in which virtually an entire population, consciously practicing freedom, are symbolically metamorphosed into beasts.

In sum, society may be construed as representing a decent, flexible mean, or as falling into the extremes of rigidity and flaccidity; as having adequate power, excessive power, or defective power; as maintaining order, practicing tyranny, or collapsing into anarchy. The drama expressing these views will be, respectively, comedy of manners, the romantic melodrama of society which exalts the individual as against the group, and the melodrama of social disaster which sees, as coevals, the decay of order in society and the drift of a triumphant individualism into an instinctivism generating herds and, in its destructive phase, mobs.

Such matters give some perspective on, and provide some context for, the placement of *The Firebugs* and *The Birthday Party*. As dramas of society, what kind of social reality do they divine? If they have also, as I believe, a strong urge to be philosophic dramas, what kind of stance do they take, and what ideas of men do they dramatically utilize? Or, similar as they are in the men and events they put on the stage, do they maintain similar stances or seem to embrace similar ideas? Are the two pairs of malevolent aggressors related? Or the victims, one burned in his house, the other taken away in a hearse-like car?

We can quickly make one assertion: neither is a comedy of manners. Both do include comic detail, witty lines, satirical shots at stupidity, banality, and self-ignorance, and, above all, the implication that the human community is more threatened by deformity in man than by conformity. They invite laughs. But the laughs are uneasy, a weak counter to dread. The plays do not include compromise, accommodation, or resolutions in which the norms retain authority and so foreshadow continuity.

Frisch is not cryptic. Schmitz and Eisenring have only one way of life, one end: destruction. They are literary anticipations of the firebomb, Molotov cocktail types, but they are full-time arsonists of relentless energy, not occasional nuisances. By giving them traditional diabolic identities, Frisch declares them not a puzzling aberration, but a permanent reality of life. That is, destructiveness is as "human" or "natural" as creativeness. It is the central diabolic mode: Mephistopheles was out to destroy Faustus, Diabolus to destroy the city of Mansoul, Satan to destroy Adam and Eve. The favorite target is the exemplary, but any going affair appeals to the dark destroying instinct. Schmitz and Eisenring act traditionally and spontaneously; they respond to their own natures, not to some inflicted pain that begets revengefulness. They do allude to grievances, but these are decor, not structure. Their action does not represent a cause-and-effect rationale, from which it follows that removal of the cause will remove the effect. Their destructiveness is not a consequence but a given. As the Ph.D. says, when he discovers that they are not the utopian radicals he had taken them for, "The one thing I didn't know was this: They—they are doing it for the pure joy of it" (scene 8).

Schmitz and Eisenring are now destroying Biedermann—good fellow, houseowner, i.e., the middle class, the bourgeoisie. True destructiveness aims at the center of social organization. There would be no point in burning down palaces, castles, museums, hovels, shanties. Schmitz and Eisenring report burning down a restaurant, a hotel, a theater, a circus—centers of popular life—but what we hear most about is the burning down of houses; that is, the wiping out of a class which owns houses, keeps servants, and has comforts and perhaps elegance. It is the class that, when it is secure in its balance and good sense and is therefore resistant to assault, provides the foundation for comedy of manners. It implies a society that siphons off enough destructiveness into duel patterns, feud patterns, and war patterns, which have different forms in different ages, to be able to treat as follies or as survivable vices the excesses and deficiencies, of intellectual and moral virtues, that keep challenging the norms. Frisch turns comedy of manners upside down: the security and vigor are all with the challengers, and the figure symbolizing society has a corner on the follies—the misunderstanding of the facts, of himself, and hence of an appropriate posture toward the facts. Ironically, the comic is still present: in his wrongheadedness Biedermann is silly, and silliness is laughable. Part of Frisch's skill is to lead us to respond as if to comedy, for this responsiveness makes the cumulative shocks more devastating. Silliness we expect to lead to embarrassment or humiliation; when the silly man capitulates to destroyers, we feel betrayed. Reminiscences of comedy of manners are another turn of the screw in the melodrama of societal disaster.

Since we have an unprecedented faith in social therapy, Frisch shocks us by showing antisocial destructiveness as a primary motive rather than a corrigible malfunction. His central shock, of course, is showing this destructiveness as successfully attacking central institutions to which we cling. Frisch may be saying that society is weak, but, if I read him aright, he is rather saying that it is vulnerable, which is a different thing. He is at pains to show that Biedermann has available the forces that symbolize institutional strength against aggression—firemen and policemen who are uncorrupted, clearsighted, and eager to act. Biedermann is vulnerable, however, because he does not call on these forces, does not make his potential strength effective in a crisis. Instead, in the play's bitterest irony, he makes love to his destroyers, the arsonists who have seized squatter's rights in his house. Among other things, *The Firebugs* says that society cannot be destroyed unless it collaborates actively with its destroyers. What it does most brilliantly, however, is analyze Biedermann's vulnerability, the reasons why he placates his destroyers, ignores his potential saviors, and even obstructs them.

For one thing, Biedermann has a skeleton in his closet: he has unjustly fired an employee, Knechtling, and Knechtling has committed suicide. Schmitz is sure Biedermann won't call the police against them "Because he's guilty himself" (scene 4), and Schmitz and Eisenring make rather subtle use of this. They keep the issue alive in Biedermann's mind by affecting to sympathize with him and by accusing Knechtling of ingratitude. Biedermann does not grasp the honorable course open to him: make what reparation he can to the Widow Knechtling, who keeps hopefully calling. Instead he in effect does penance, futilely and monstrously, by putting himself in the hands of killers. Society need not purge its guilt by committing suicide.

Biedermann, furthermore, is immobilized by more commonplace urgencies. As the Chorus says, he "dreads action / More than disaster" (scene 4); he wants "peace and quiet" (scene 4, scene 5). He appears to know that his visitors are scoundrels, but he fears that, if he makes enemies of them by calling the police, he cannot do business as usual (scene 5). When the firemen press him about what is going on in his attic, where the arsonists have installed cans of gasoline and wires for detonation, he treats them as if they were government inquisitors interfering in a private house (scene 4). So he tries not to believe what he sees. Schmitz and Eisenring help him in this by telling him the truth and joking about it, for, as Eisenring candidly tells Biedermann, the truth and jests are the best camouflage of a plot (scene 5). Biedermann finally stakes all on "appeasing" them (by a big dinner which is a last supper), and he comes up with various familiar justifications. We need a "little trust in people," he says, and the Chorus says he hopes "that goodness / Will come of goodness" (scene 4). He urges a "little good will," a "little idealism"; he believes in "the natural goodness of man" (scene 5). He is, as the Chorus laments, "Tough in business / But rather soft of heart" (scene 4).

Hence the rich assortment of fatal ironies: his will to disbelieve the truth; his search for an easy way out; his misapplication of ethical hortatives; his taking of half-truths for eternal verities. These surround a central irony which is a basic source of the sinister tone: Biedermann's initial vulner-ability—it first lets Schmitz get a foot in the door and then keeps increasing the difficulty of throwing him and Eisenring out—lies in his acting on values of the highest repute in our day. Schmitz and Eisenring skillfully force him into the style of the good man of his time. Seeking entry, Schmitz craves only "kindness" and "humanity." Once in, he tells Bieder-mann, "This country needs men like you, sir. . . . You have a conscience." He praises Biedermann for not throwing him out: "*That's* what we need, Mr. Biedermann! Humanity!" (scene 2). He is all for "Private charity" and laments that "everything [is] State-controlled. No real people left, . . ." (scene 3). And when it appears that the police are calling—possible rescuers, the audience knows—he complains, "It's the Police State!" (scene 5). Biedermann cannot buck this cliché. Even less can he resist the self-pity of the intruders, who candidly admit that "sentiment" is one of their major devices of camouflage and who come up with every cliché of the underprivileged life; Schmitz, in Eisenring's stock phrase, was only a "football of fate" (scene 8). Schmitz first appears when it is raining outside. He is "unemployed" and has "no place to sleep." But he is "used to sleeping on the floor," for "father was a miner" (scene 2). Because of the "old days in the mines" he is used to "starving and freezing"; he had learned no manners, as "they used to tell me at the orphan-age." He appears to have such hurt feelings that even skepti-cal Mrs. Biedermann bursts out, "You had an unfortunate childhood—." Schmitz tops it: "No childhood at all, madam. . . . My mother died when I was seven," and he wipes his eyes (scene 3). Eisenring voices the popular cliché: ". . . his youth was tragic" (scene 5).

In such details we see a drama of our own society. Schmitz and Eisenring can be read, if one chooses, as the Communists in the government of President Beneš or as the Nazis [3] who haunted Frisch's imagination (cf. *Count Oederland* and *Andorra*). Such a reading would be too narrow, however, for Frisch has so generalized them that they are wholly recognizable in America now. Besides, the drama of men is also a drama of man; the play about society is also a morality play. Biedermann is openly called Everyman, and Schmitz and Eisenring are, in the end, ahistorical. They are the incurable destructiveness that lurks in mankind, the ultimate evil that in each age diabolically seeks the vulnerable spot. Frisch's best insight is into the kinship between vulnerability and virtue: the true destroyer gets at man through the imperatives of his day, for in his innocence man has not learned, or in his hubris is unwilling, to qualify them. Lucifer would attack Salem by being the best of witch-hunters, Sparta by being the best of ascetic disciplinarians. In our time his role must be that of the victim of society, rubbing society's nose in its guilt, calling on its humanity, and crying out against the police state.

Pinter's Goldberg and McCann are destroyers too. But they do away only with Stanley Webber, the Boleses' roomer. The Boles house remains intact; the Boleses live on. Meg, sentimental and imperceptive, is going to undergo at least a disappointment. Petey, however, has undergone a disenchantment; if nothing more, he will be painfully sadder and wiser. In a reversal of a traditional situation, the young man's disaster is the old man's initiation. Petey, in his sixties plays Nick Adams to the Ole Andreson of Stanley Webber, in his thirties. The analogy is only partial, however; for Petey's voice is not central, the stage belongs principally to the Mephistophelian visitants and their victim, and the situation lacks the unambiguousness of Hemingway's "The Killers." Still, there is a victim who expects and dreads visitors and who stays in the house; and the visitors take over with a strange authority, derived, as it may be, from powerful weapons or a merciless code.

Looked at as a drama of society, *The Birthday Party* portrays neither the triumph nor the destruction of an existent order, but a breach and a violation of it. Stanley is not made a heroic figure, but when he is taken away, the society represented in the Boles household is diminished. It has lost something of value, perhaps because of its own deficiencies of being or tactics. It may also be that some other order has better claims: Stanley must move elsewhere, to follow a destiny or undergo a penalty from which there is no sanctuary. The pattern may be that of the feud or of rival realms: competing orders of undetermined validity. Or Goldberg and McCann may be the agents of some underground suborder preying on society, a parasitic Mafia with its quasi order threatening general order. Certainly the gangland murder is what comes first to mind.

If Stanley is simply being rubbed out, for unspecified irregularities, then Pinter has shown enormous ingenuity in translating mobster action into verbal and psychological terms. These killers have no guns; their threats can pass as grotesque humor; they seem partners in a fantastic charade. They arrive casually, looking for a room; Goldberg chats about his past; jovial and outgoing, he is a big party type and is quickly setting up the birthday party for Stanley. The sinister enters indirectly in Stanley's fear of them and in their mysterious assurance and power (like that of Schmitz and Eisenring in Frisch's play), as the air of fun and games in no way conceals an ominous concentration on a murky goal. Twice, however, their steady, almost hypnotic compulsion of Stanley breaks out into a sadistic barrage of questions, charges, and vilifications; with its rapid-fire, rat-a-tat-tat stichomythy, this is like machinegun fire transmuted into psychic attack. At the end, what might be the dead body of the victim is still alive physically, all dressed up, though moving with difficulty and issuing only incoherent sounds. Instead of death we have death-in-life, spiritual debility. All this is brilliantly original—a transposition into another key of traditional melodramatic actions such as the enemy's commando raid, the feudist's snatch, the mob's kidnapping and wiping out.

However, to translate Pinter's masterful and terrifying fable back into these commoner terms may seem reductive, as if beneath fresh and inventive decor lay only banality of motivation. Another possible reading makes Goldberg and McCann into less commonplace assassins: they are carrying out a ritual murder. This view is attractive because it takes account of the air of mystery that hangs over the proceedings; it suggests the mysteries, the arcane realm of belief and practice that penetrates, it lets us feel, to some special reality. Death is not a penalty or some other explicable consequence but an imperative, a compelling ceremonial; the victim is mere object in a sacred process. Thus Goldberg and McCann again resemble Schmitz and Eisenring, at least to the extent that both destructively enact a way of life outside the usual human bonds.

So far, however, we have not looked at the kind of person Stanley Webber is. It is possible that he is not merely a neutral victim of a rite, or a man who "asked for it" or seemed to invite his fate (by being a dropout from the party, an apostate, a political refugee, a suspect of some kind, or even a sick man who has fled a sanitarium). On the face of it Stanley is a mild, rather unaggressive person whom it is difficult to imagine arousing strong antagonism. The text makes much, however, of two attributes of his: his career, real or imagined, as a pianist, and his glasses. In act 1 Meg says she liked to watch him play, and she wonders when he will play again professionally; he gives an account, possibly a fantasy, of a big concert in the past and a big offer for the future; during the inquisition by Goldberg and McCann he says that his "trade" is playing the piano. Suppose, then, we think of Stanley as an artist,[4] whether potential or manqué: the attacks of Goldberg and McCann take on a slightly different air. Who is hostile to the artist and wants to control him? Traditionally, the regime that will be damaged by his insights, be it a political tyranny or a rigid, fearful society. Hence the drum episode is very meaningful. On the one hand Meg gives Stanley the drum because she wants to revive him as musician (his piano is mysteriously missing). On the other hand, when Stanley is "it" during a game of blindman's buff, McCann so places the drum that Stanley steps on it and breaks it. The heart of McCann's dirty trick is the silencing of the artist even in a secondary medium, and the trick is a key event in the defining of Goldberg and McCann.

With the drum business in mind, we find the drama of Stanley's glasses significant in a very specific way. In act 1, four passages, pretty well spaced out, make us especially aware of the glasses and of their importance to Stanley. Hence, when Goldberg and McCann, giving Stanley the third degree in act 2, snatch his glasses, what might be only a routine application of pressure seems rather to be a special attack on his independent vision. His powers of resistance weaken, he screams, and he is hardly more than a cipher at the end of the birthday party which immediately follows. At the party itself the glasses symbolism is expanded in several ways. Twice, to accompany toasts to Stanley, McCann turns off the lights and shines a flashlight directly in Stanley's face, as if to single him out for honor, like the spotlighted star in a show; a further step in the torture, this is another way of blinding him. Then Goldberg approves a suggestion that they play blindman's buff: McCann, who is "it," "touches Stanley's glasses," making Stanley "it"; to blindfold Stanley, McCann takes his glasses. Then McCann takes two hostile actions, one significantly right after the other: he "breaks Stanley's glasses, snapping the frames," and he puts the drum where Stanley steps on it and breaks it. Stanley is to be permanently blinded—by excess of other men's light—and cut off from his musical vocation. Suddenly there comes the third and final blackout—this time the meter needs a shilling—and with it a general turmoil of ignorant bodies clashing by night. Finally Goldberg and McCann get hold of the flashlight and again turn it on Stanley's face, pursuing him with it as he giggles hysterically in an apparent crack-up.

At this point we detect only a ruthless attempt to put the artist—his special talents, and the insights associated with his calling—out of business. But a much more cunning and more calculating scheme appears in act 3, when Goldberg and McCann are getting ready to take Stanley, now in a state of "breakdown," away in their "big car." We learn that Stanley is trying to put on his broken glasses; Petey wants to help fix the frames with tape, but Goldberg vetoes this. He will not permit Stanley the disinterested help by which he might recover his own vision. Instead Goldberg and McCann promise to "buy him another pair." They make a strong issue of this: "it's about time you had a new pair of glasses"; "You can't see straight"; "You've been cockeyed for years." This you-better-see-things-our-way line introduces the second stichomythic pressure passage, where our attention is first caught by a revealing stage direction: "They begin to woo him, gently and with relish." They first tell him, in various images, what bad shape he is in; then they say "But we can save you" and shift into a rush of glowing promises in which every reader must recognize the hackneyed seductions of the world that has something to sell: use the club bar—keep a table reserved—free pass—hot tips—day and night service— all on the house—adjusted—a success—integrated. As Stanley's "hands clutching his glasses begin to tremble," they keep pressing him, with salesmen's mercilessness, to approve "the prospect"—the view, the scene, the look ahead (they use the word five times). Their business is to compel him to see things as they do—to serve them. In a word, they are the crass commercial society—of sales, blandishments, guarantees, and profits material and psychological—demanding that the artist give up his role as seer and buy its own way of looking at things. Then he can help sell.

With this in mind, we can look more understandingly at the machine-gun scene (act 2) in which Goldberg and McCann mount their first assult on Stanley. Here they do not promise; they only challenge, accuse, abuse. Precisely: the first step in bringing someone into line is to break down resistance by producing a conviction, if not of sin, at least of inadequacy, incompetence, poor judgment, bad habits, and miscellaneous questionable conduct. As always, Goldberg and McCann pump out a flood of clichés (which Pinter invests with great dramatic life, just as he does the banalities and non-sequiturs of Meg). Their barrage of questions embraces the world of ads and commercials accusing mankind of bad breath, body odor, and hidden ailments to set him up for buying soap, perfume, and patent medicine. However, their cross-examination also includes implicit charges of political, intellectual, and religious shortcomings, as if other institutions besides the cash-nexus society were pressing the disciplinary inquisition of the perceptive individual. The charge that is emphasized by repetition is "betrayal," climaxed in McCann's "Judas." This could of course apply to anybody who is out of line with going styles of behavior and feeling, but it makes especial sense as applied to the artist, who is characteristically thought of as critic and deflator of the way of his own world.

But the way of the world is powerful. As we go back to the beginning and notice Stanley's fear of the announced visitors, we can read it as fear of his own weakness before worldly pressures. Yet at the same time he is felt by Goldberg and McCann to be a special job: in pounding people into the deformity that results from conformity to an incomplete pattern of life, the enforcers find ordinary men easier subjects than artists, who more often resist and rebel. The rebellious impulse appears symbolically in Stanley at the end of act 1 when he plays the drum, "his face and the drumbeat now savage and possessed." He understands the birthday party: "just . . . another booze-up," "plain stupid." He tries to throw Goldberg and McCann out. They are "nothing but a dirty joke." He himself feels "responsibility toward the people in this house. . . . They've lost their sense of smell." (Cf. the remark of the Chorus Leader in *The Firebugs* when Biedermann says he doesn't smell the gasoline in the house: "How soon he's got accustomed to bad smells!" [scene 4].) His will to resist endures surprisingly; even after an extended third degree he kicks Goldberg in the stomach. When blindfolded he apparently tries to strangle Meg (act 2). Just as he is being taken away at the end, Goldberg says, "He needs special treatment," as if even now their conversion of him were not a sure thing (act 3). Goldberg and McCann have shown considerable irascibility and tension (which would be worth analysis in itself), as if their task had strained even their powers.

Potentially strong as he is, Stanley seems doomed either to servitude to Goldberg and McCann or to dependence on

Meg, the sexy-motherly lodginghouse keeper who, with her crush on him, is both attentive and bossy. As Meg's lodger, Stanley the artist is kept-man of the women's clubs, protégé of the vast female society that pursues culture and "loves art." As non-seeing and nonsense-speaking creature of Gold- berg and McCann, he is slave of a mass culture that blares out strident clichés through brazen mass media. Pinter seems to say that Stanley has only a choice between a demanding vulgar, promotional world and a demanding sentimental, indulgent one. Still, Meg wants him to resume his career; and there is another kind of hope in Petey, who plays chess instead of going to the birthday party, who provides the shilling that turns on the light again, who likes Stanley and does not push him around, and who would keep him out of the hands of Goldberg and McCann if he could. The scarcely hidden persuaders push Petey around too. But he is not corrupted.

It is significant that at the birthday party there is great rapport between Meg and the visitors; she simply finds a great good time at the party which to them is an instrument of their mission. The woman who fondles the artist and the culture which would use him have some common ground. The party where their games mesh is a very suggestive one. It is reminiscent of the publisher's or art-dealer's promotional cocktail party, of the public or social occasion where the artist is made much of, of the "entertainment" for a "pros- pect." It implies that he falls in rather than rebels, goes along rather than goes his own way (blinded, dazzled, speechless, but still perhaps reluctant). Yet as a birthday party it also implies an ironic rebirth—a rebirth into the world that is having its way. Stanley enters the world all dressed up in striped trousers, black jacket, and white collar, and carrying a bowler hat—the costume of one making it in the world. The "big car" can very well be that of success. It is often taken to be a funeral car. There is no reason why it cannot be taken both ways at once: for one kind of man, death and the world may be identical. And if the world implies slavery, we can think of Stanley as playing Lucky to Goldberg and McCann's Pozzo.

In this reading, then, *The Birthday Party* exemplifies the

romantic melodrama of men: society oppresses the individual of special talent and insight. Its method of oppression is to coordinate him, bring him into line, use him. And yet *The Birthday Party* really represents society in three aspects—the supersalesmen who pound the individual into insensibility with the day's minatory and promissory clichés, the mistress-and-mother who will sponge on him and yet jog him as sonny-boy-friend, and, on the other hand, in Petey, the quiet undominating friend who would give comfort and aid but who cannot prevail against the predators. So the tendency is somewhat away from the morality play, where man takes on a monolithic quality, and toward a realistic multiplicity of men. Still the action centers on Goldberg and McCann, a dual Mr. Worldly Wiseman with power and the single-minded will to enforce it. Morality play yes, but with a difference. Pinter's skill is to translate the power of the world into gangster idiom, the ordinary public brainwashing by mass media into an extraordinary domestic third degree. The sinister lies in a fusion that simultaneously exacts incompatible responses—that to the oppressive society of Ibsen, and that to the antisocial conspiratorial gunmen. This is analogous to Frisch's method in *The Firebugs*, which fuses, in one pair, the appeal to compassion and the evocation of the dread of total destruction. The sinisterly powerful pairs in the two plays, however, mark alternative extremes possible to the melodrama of social disaster: the destruction of the individual by oppressive order (the older tradition), and the elimination of order by the destructive instinct (the newer vision). The devil can happily work it either way.

The Upward Path
Notes on the Work of Katherine Anne Porter [1]

HOWARD BAKER

"The Downward Path to Wisdom" is the title of one of Katherine Anne Porter's most characteristic short stories.[2] In it a boy, still almost a baby, comes into an elementary consciousness of himself and the world. He begins to realize that he is a thing apart from other things, something named Stephen; as for the world, he recapitulates an ancient discovery, to the effect that human beings, as such, are bad. "I hate Mama," he chants as the story closes, "I hate Papa, I hate Grandma, I hate Uncle David, I hate old Janet, I hate Marjory." It's a sort of litany that he has made up, not too unreasonably, after some exhausting, vainglorious, and utterly humiliating first adventures, and he chants it to himself with quiet satisfaction, even while he is falling asleep, cuddled against his mother's knee. The story of his experience, admittedly, adds up to a somewhat darkish paradox.

That the path to wisdom has to be like that, downward, is an observation which Heraclitus appears first to have written into the record quite a few centuries ago. This notion, along with an array of similar sentiments, got Heraclitus the nickname "the weeping philosopher"; and because he also said that the downward path is likewise the upward path the Ancients decided to describe him further as "Heraclitus the obscure," and taking into account the whole range of his opinions, "Heraclitus the dark." In the popular simplifications he was a pessimist, an iconoclast, an utterer of impenetrable truths; and conversely a scorner of plain cheap laughable things.

Just such another is Katherine Anne Porter. A maker of darkish parables, a producer of wines as dry as wines ever ought to be, she has proved hard to deal with, except in simplistic terms such as those applied to Heraclitus. For years she was praised by discerning critics as the cleanest, clearest, and as they say of vines, most shy-bearing of the writers of our times: which in my opinion she probably is. Then, after writing the best seller *Ship of Fools* (1962), she came to be regarded in wider circles with a certain uneasiness, as being negative, skeptical, prejudiced, formalistic: which in my opinion she is not. She is no more negative, I must argue, no more skeptical, et cetera, than it is very good to be.

I intend to look at her work with the hope of tracing out some of the downward paths (which are also upward paths) that lead to her peculiar wisdom. In order to pin things down as much as possible, I'll make some remarks by way of comment on a handful of critical pieces that deal with her and will have their inevitable effect on her repute as a writer.[3]

Two propositions will be of leading importance. One is that Miss Porter is a Modern, a beneficiary of a discipline which has been known as Modernism, just as surely as any of a number of writers who can be grouped together because of their affinities with James and Proust and Joyce. She is akin to Ezra Pound and Pablo Picasso. She grew up in a period in which the mastery of an art was held to be a lifelong, exacting discipline. It was a period, we can say from this distance, which accepted constraints and past history, as well as freedom and modernity.

The other proposition is that a span of some ten formative years spent living in the bosom of a civilization different from our own, situated on a different level on the anthropological timetable, must have a drastic effect on the development of a writer. To be sure it was common for writers to live abroad in the twenties; it was common too for a number of them to show up in Mexico and to stay there for months or years; but I think few of them ever crept into the genius of an archaic people the way Katherine Anne Porter did at the very beginning of her career, and, to her advantage, never really extricated herself from it.

James Joyce's *Dubliners*, Miss Porter has said, was for her, as a young beginning writer, a revelation. She was contrasting herself, in a little essay on Willa Cather,[4] with Miss Cather, whose work she admired within limits and whose literary origins she respected while recognizing them as being very different from her own, in that they had nothing of the "modern" implicit in them. For her it was otherwise; she had apprenticed herself in the school of James Joyce, and having acknowledged so much, she instantly excluded Gertrude Stein from it on the grounds that "tricky techniques and disordered syntax" did not properly belong in the category of the art to which she was referring. No, it was quite simply in the art of Joyce's small collection of insights into Dublin lives, with their matchless unpretentious clarity, their evasive surfaces and depths, that she felt she took her start as a modern writer.

Reading through all of her stories again, the old ones along with four that have been reprinted in the *Collected Stories* (1965), leaves me with a fresh sense of the kinship with Joyce. Things ranging from the white palsied hands of the stricken priest in Joyce's first story to the universal snowfall at the end of the last one, have their counterparts on Miss Porter's pages. These are highly emotional things, parts of common human experience, rich sweeping passages in no way tricked up with rhetorical devices, though always true to the irresistible imperatives of art.

In comparison with kinship, I can't take the theory of direct borrowing, as expounded lately, very seriously. A pre-possession with influence as evidenced by borrowed details has become a trademark in scholarly studies. It is conspicuous in George Hendrick's useful study, *Katherine Anne Porter*, in which he assembles bibliographical materials and pertinent excerpts from other critics along with his own excellent running survey of her work. We all will agree with him that Miss Porter probably got a sense of tone from the beginning of *A Portrait of the Artist as a Young Man* which helped her with the story "The Downward Path to Wisdom." But we will reflect on two things. Joyce adopted the intonations of childhood only to be in a position to change

them as his story develops; Miss Porter adopts an intonation
in order to sustain it—and to make it uniquely her own as
she takes the story around full circle, as is perfectly clear in
her reading of it on a commercially issued phonograph record. As for the name *Stephen*, which is common to both
pieces of fiction, rather than indicating dependence on Joyce,
or the ordinary sort of derivation from him, it may be
standing there as an open tribute to an admired predecessor,
a way of saying thanks for things much more important, and
much harder to explicate. When it comes to sifting through
a text hunting for significant names, puns, images, symbols
and so on, the results, to my eye, look grotesque sometimes. I
can't imagine by what process of mind Frances, the name of
the little girl in the story, would have to be suggested by the
country to which Stephen Dedalus exiles himself—unless
this is suggested facetiously.

The revelation that came to her with her first reading of
Dubliners, Miss Porter goes on to say, could hardly have
happened except to a very young writer *"with some preparation of mind by the great literature of the past."* Those are
my italics; I put them there because I believe the statement
is the crux in any effective account of Modernism. In regard
to the bearing of some of the great achievements of the past
on her own development, Miss Porter has been about as
forthright as anyone can be. We can name some of the
authors who interested her greatly. But perhaps we can
clarify the whole matter most easily by considering first what
a preparation of mind by great literature meant, what it
consisted in, during the first decades of the century.

Let's consider Joyce and his own preparations. We know
from the *Portrait of the Artist as a Young Man* that the
author of *Dubliners*, on the verge of exile from home and
faith, was ravaged by the spectral grandeurs of Aristotle and
Aquinas, fascinated by Latinity in general, and delighted by
the songs of the Elizabethans. As for the Elizabethans: "His
mind, in the vesture of a doubting monk, stood often in the
shadow under the windows of that age, to hear the grave and
mocking music of the lutenists." If we should imagine that
not much of this shows in his stories of Dublin, we would be

wrong; Joyce's mind stands in the shadow, under Dublin windows, always in the vesture of the doubting monk. We know from *Ulysses* what other windows his mind stood under. Greek windows, for the main part. And later under the collapsed porticoes of many literatures, in *Finnegans Wake*, simultaneously. But central to everything else was the epic of the wanderings of Odysseus. No doubt the ultimate preparation of Joyce's mind was to be found in the classics of antiquity.

And so, hypothetically, we may suppose that Katherine Anne Porter also moved from her deceptively lucid stories laid in recognizable backgrounds to the more elaborate and more studiously imaginative projections in *Ship of Fools*—whose affinities with the literature of the past are also at once recognizable and concealed.

In any event she was writing those first stories at a time of fresh responsiveness to the distant past. The head of Nefertiti became almost as familiar during those years as the face of Dorothy Gish, and Louis Armstrong was singing about the joys and sorrows of old King Tut. Troy and Mycenae, and Helen and Menelaus and Agamemnon, became historical fixtures, not merely the stuff of myth. Sir Arthur Evans was digging up the palace of Minos, while Joyce was turning the epigraph for the *Portrait of the Artist* over in his mind: "Et ignotas animum dimitti in artes"—Ovid's words for Daedalus's determination to escape from Minos's Crete by bending his genius toward unknown arts. Picasso, along with Diaghilev and Cocteau, found himself in Southern Italy in 1917, looking at genuine Greek art, with such profound and lasting effect that eventually he formed the habit of assigning certain paintings of his to Antipolis, rather than to Antibes, where he was officially residing.

Miss Porter's contemporaries and friends were busy establishing their own exchanges with periods removed from their own. T. S. Eliot, who had not yet entered openly into his theological program, was at his best, in my opinion, when he was transposing classicism into an Elizabethan rhetoric that was full of burnished thrones and Ionian red and gold. W. B. Yeats, though no longer young, apprenticed himself to the goldsmiths of Byzantium. Allen Tate began insisting with polite stubbornness on the validity of the later Roman myths. Caroline Gordon studied how to conceal the echoes of Greek tragedy that she was hearing in her head. Yvor Winters met the unmitigated ferocity of the well-known Greek myths face to face, head to head . . . at exactly the time that he was printing one of Miss Porter's ferocious, bland-sounding stories, "Theft," in the little handmade magazine called the *Gyroscope*.

But Ezra Pound is the best case in point. "In Mexico many years ago," Katherine Anne Porter wrote in 1950, "Hart Crane and I were reading again *Pavannes and Divisions*, and at some dogmatic statement in the text Crane suddenly burst out: 'I'm tired of Ezra Pound!' And I asked him: 'Well who else is there?' He thought a few seconds and said: 'It's true there's nobody like him, anybody to take his place.' "

Looking back from this distance we can imagine that as a bully, a rapaciously well-read and singularly gifted bully, nobody could have taken his place in forcing a certain kind of classicism on a fairly dull literary world. And not by noisy precept alone, but by superb example. In Pound's "Homage to Sextus Propertius" we all shared, in those days, in the recovery of something unexpectedly beautiful, something somewhat similar to Picasso's pen-and-ink Greek drawings, something at once new and old, with none of the stale evils of neoclassicism hanging over it.

Pound's gift consisted partly in recognizing the power of the new and unfamiliar intertwined among the old. In the case of Propertius he was dealing with a poet who was especially well schooled in the pagan elegiac arts and attitudes of the early Greeks; in translating fragments of him he cleared the way for a view of beauties which lay somewhat outside the normal Western Anglo-Saxon experience, but which, once seen, could then be recognized on the pages of more familiar texts; and thus a part of the *Odyssey* underwent a renewal in "Canto I." In a word Pound led in a renaissance not simply of pre-Christian literature, but of pre-Classical as well.

Katherine Anne Porter goes on in the essay from which I have quoted to analyze with great lucidity—she is notably intelligent as a critic—the disaster which eventually overtook a great poet. By degrees Pound persuaded himself, she says, really to hate the principal institutions in the Western Anglo-Saxon world, so exclusively had become his dedication to the old Mediterranean world; and along with hatred of institutions, persons. He condemned Jews, but—and this is Miss Porter's main point—he condemned Christians as such just as savagely: he had become a determined polytheist in his heart and mind. Her point is well taken. The root of Pound's belligerence is to be found, I should say, in the utter disillusionment expressed in the lines in "Hugh Selwyn Mauberley" describing civilization as it looked to him during World War I: "An old bitch gone in the teeth."

This topic has considerable bearing on Miss Porter's own work. No one will venture to read much complacency toward our institutions, or toward the persons charged with running them, into what she has to say in her fiction. To the contrary, in her view people would have to seem to be bad, if measured against any abstract standards of good and evil; *hoi pleistoi kakoi*, as we said, would seem to be nearer to her kind of truth. But if so it must be, then it does not follow that there is in it something to be sodden and truculent about. The Greek phrase is simply an old pre-Socratic observation, attributed to Heraclitus's neighbor, Bias of Priene. It is at once pleasantly Ionian and wisely archaic. Ezra Pound seems to have misused its substance in the same heavy-handed way that he often misused colloquial speech in his informal writings.

Nor ought we minimize the force of the pre-Christian, pre-Classical state of mind on the minds of the Moderns. "The Downward Path to Wisdom" could hardly have occurred as a title without the widespread reevaluation of ancient philosophy that was going on earlier this century. Heraclitean fragments, rescued from scattered ancient texts, assembled and published, made their inevitable impact. The unending flux of things, the tension of the deadly twanging bowstring and the sweetly singing lyre-string—bespoke a more than ordinary knowledge of beauty and destruction, life and death. And on top of all that, there was for once a completely unambiguous disdain for the second-rate. "To me," Heraclitus said, "one man is ten thousand if he be best." Standards had become high; and with high standards there always go concomitant risks.

The risks could be observed on every side. Katherine Anne Porter's friend and fellow workman in the arts, Hart Crane, took the risks and succumbed to them. Although cause and effect are difficult to determine here, it appears that for Crane an insight into civilizations earlier than ours—perhaps as depicted in the limp leather Modern Library volumes of Friedrich Nietzsche—may have intensified both his strange new poetics and his destructive Dionysiac raptures; there is still much to be puzzled out about him, as a glance at L. S. Dembo's *Hart Crane's Sanskrit Charge* will reveal.

In any event, Hart Crane arrived in Mexico as the guest of Miss Porter in 1931, but soon departed from her company and her conversation and roared away drunk until he found the ship from which he could throw himself off, into the sea, while she was preparing to move on to Europe, patiently reconciling herself to the thirty years of sobriety that it would take to investigate what life would look like if examined closely, as for instance in the microcosm of a ship.

"I write about Mexico," she wrote in 1923, when she had in fact written very little about anything, "because that is my familiar country." In 1965, forty-two years later, in the preface of what will have to be one of the two great products of her lifetime, the *Collected Stories*, she stresses the fact that her first stories were all of Mexico, "my much-loved second country." Hers was a long engagement to the second country. The reasons she gave in 1923 for her love of Mexico—her home was in South Texas, and her father, having gone down there in his youth, told enchanting tales about the country; she was attracted to the revolution; she wanted to study "the renascence of Mexican art"—are no doubt true reasons as far as they go. But when suddenly in the midst of a sentence she starts trying to say how Mexico actually was for her, she

begins revealing the depth, and the very truth, of her attach-
ment:

During the Madero revolution I watched a street battle between
Maderistas and Federal troops from the window of a cathedral;
a grape-vine heavy with tiny black grapes formed a screen, and
a very old Indian woman stood near me, perfectly silent, holding
my sleeve.

The awareness of this second human being, this older other
one, silently clutching a sleeve and watching the deadly
fighting in the street from another angle of history, will make
the great difference in the development of the writer.

"María Concepción," her first story (1922), relates the
multicolored history of another small but deadly battle, and
of the acceptances with which the Indians concerned with it
allowed it to terminate. María Concepción murders her rival.
But neither the authority of the law nor the mandates of the
church will persuade anyone to give evidence against her. To
the contrary everyone, including the wayward gamecock she
was married to, undertakes spontaneously to protect her. The
conflict is between unlovely, black-and-white justice on the
one hand, and on the other certain evasive things, like a day
full of the golden shimmer of honey bees, like the flamboy-
ant by-play of seduction, the stain of blood on a bright
chemise, fields and thorns and nursing infants—passion and
timeless pastoral life. Against these latter forces the demands
of the former abstractions are not allowed to prevail. The
community is content to look on with an ambiguous archaic
smile. The necessary lesson of the *Oresteia*, that justice dare
not be left to the discretion of the injured, is for the moment
suppressed.

The power of this extraordinary story comes from its
insight into what is clearly a pre-Aeschylean mode of order-
ing the events of life. It heightens the sense of the remote
rightness of Indian ways, and of the dry inadequacy that may
be more or less inherent in ways opposed to theirs: our ways.
We are obliged as readers to see things we take for granted
overturned. Nothing momentous is being proved to us of
course; nothing like a clear distinction between right and

wrong; but then I don't imagine that Aeschylus, in taking the contrary point of view, thought that he was proving anything either. Art is longer than the life of a social doctrine.

The first story gives the pattern for much that is to be found in Miss Porter's fiction, from first to last. And well it should, because the pattern is elemental. María Concepción is another Antigone. Both women can triumph over the almost irresistible mechanism of organized society because, in their weakness and simplicity, they harken back to fundamental imperatives. Justice and social authority, subject as they are to constant hardening, and constant distorting to suit the pleasure of the man or party in power, stand in constant need of apology. Plato worked at one type of apology, Aristotle at another; but not with impeccable success, as Benjamin Farrington has just got through saying quite clearly, with a new pertinence, in a book on Epicurus. Complacency with regard to the best of our devices for keeping order brings them gradually to a state of paralysis.

Miss Porter's archaic world has much that is restorative to show to us. Since it is continually a frame of reference for her art, I am going to quote at a little length from the beginning of "Hacienda," familiar though the page may be. The implications as to the difference between Kennerly and the Indians are what I want to expose to view, and how complex the author's appreciations.

It was worth the price of a ticket to see Kennerly take possession of the railway train among a dark inferior people. . . . He strode mightily through, waving his free arm, lunging his portfolio and leather bag, stiffening his nostrils as conspicuously as he could against the smell that "poured," he said, "simply poured like mildewed pea soup!" from the teeming clutter of wet infants and draggled turkeys and indignant baby pigs and food baskets and bundles of vegetables and bales and hampers of domestic goods, each little mountain of confusion yet drawn into a unit, from the midst of which its owners glanced up casually from dark pleased faces at the passing strangers. . . . Almost nothing can disturb their quiet ecstasy when they are finally settled among their plunder, and the engine, mysteriously and powerfully animated, draws them lightly over the miles they have so often counted step by step. And they are not troubled by the noisy white man because, by now, they are accustomed to him.

Kennerly, in another age, might have been an adventuring *tyrannos*, like Antigone's uncle, or Plato's friend and disciple, Dion of Syracuse. But the people huddling together among the disorderly fixtures of their households are to be numbered among the poorer voyagers and migrants of any age on any continent, just as the statuettes being dug up in Morelia are of a family with the little clay figures that can be found in Syria. It's a big family of course, but it has its common purposes.

Let's generalize. Let's say as everyone has always been fond of saying, that the world goes through its several ages. I am wondering, however, whether these wouldn't be best described as a sequence moving from the primitive to the archaic to the rationalizing. The primitive is mostly very bad dreams, as Giorgio de Chirico knew and D. H. Lawrence never quite found out; the archaic has its smiling forms, but in the smiles there is often an element of cruelty; the rationalizing, unfortunately, gets itself locked in its arbitrary, often self-destructive ideologies. Art, and writing is an art, may be at its best when it stays more or less in touch with the archaic state of mind, no longer roiled with fears, and not yet deaf to everything except its own program. And of course any deterministic view of things ceases to be fully deterministic when its secret powers are brought to light, and that's somehow to be equated with the role of consciousness in all human pursuits.

It is Kennerly's imprisonment in his program, with the various imprisonments of the others who surround him in theirs, that make up the spiderweb structure of "Hacienda." The web is at its most visible when it is seen reflected in the eyes of the natives, as observed by the narrator. Once, in the *Southern Review*, thirty or more years ago, failing to realize this, I said the story seemed inconclusive. Now I do not think so. And I also see "Noon Wine," as will come out in a moment, in sharper definition now than I did then.

The poignant reversals of hope which went along with the

Mexican revolution are measured in somewhat the same way in several other early stories. Braggioni in "Flowering Judas," like so many public figures in Miss Porter's work, has suddenly attained the prerogative of rationalizing his preferences publicly and making his rationalizations stick. One can think of him as belonging to the pack of professional patriots, those in "Pale Horse, Pale Rider," for instance; unnerving fellows, all of them. But when Braggioni breaks down, he can retreat in tears to the archaic landscape provided for him by his wife. His counterpart's plight, Laura's plight, is that she is able, now and then, and finally in her dream, to begin just barely to see through her own rationalizing, but can do nothing about it. She has no archaic scenes to retreat to, try as she will in her horrible dream to whip something up out of Christian imagery. She is peculiarly alone. She resembles the passengers in *Ship of Fools*; at sea and finding it hard to go to sleep.

As for the Christian imagery in this story, I think that, contrary to much that has been written about it—see George Hendrick's summary—there is no specific virtue in it. The Judas-betrayal form of Laura's dream seems to me to mean mostly that she has betrayed herself. She has failed to discover an Other one through whose eyes she can see herself; and in particular she goes through the motions of living with the native people, seeing them every day and teaching their children, without seeing them at all.

Certainly a retreat into Arcadia or into the religious visions of childhood, or into Freudian psychoanalysis or anything of that sort, would hardly appear to be Miss Porter's notion of a solution to the problems she brings up. Despite its fine clarity the archaic mode of life eludes those who turn directly toward it, just as the rainbow which was heaven in Miranda's dream quickly eluded her. The value of the knowledge of these things remains, but they themselves have gone. Poor Juan, the great butterfly who married María Concepción, ends by rendering with regrets his eight hours a day, day after day, to his employer. He treads his own downward path to wisdom. Laborious and painful, the life of the rational man.

"Noon Wine" is a tragedy, in the ancient sense of the term, produced and staged according to the norms of modern prose fiction. The norms are used to good effect. The countenance and speech and mentality and heartbeat of Southern Texas are exposed simply and economically, and uniquely; the heartbeat is parallel with and different from that to be heard at other places, Mexico, New York, Germany. . . . And the story is only one of several that end with death. Yet this one is distinctly tragedy, perhaps for reasons in addition to the perfect objectivity with which the downfall of Mr. Thompson is told.

The house in the story sits among the ragweed, behind a broken gate, as hopeless as a primitive hut in the midst of its garbage heap; and the inhabitants of the house, the man (Mr. Thompson) and the woman and their grubby boys, are as squalid in their day-to-day purposes as savages are likely to be in theirs. But to them comes the stranger, like Demeter or Apollo in the *Hymns*, disguised. Mr. Helton is no god; he is a pale, skinny Swede; nevertheless he has strange powers, which he conceals, and also a past. He works at redeeming the farmstead, playing a little tune, a drinking tune, "Noon Wine," on a mouth organ when he is resting, and showing an ability to go now and then into a glittering rage. In due course—one would hardly be able to say how or when it was taking place—the farm, under Mr. Helton's unnoticed care, takes on a certain order, and begins, for all its rough spots, to make sense; life attains a poise, which I hope it will not be too tiresome of me to call archaic.

Then, after nine years, Mr. Hatch shows up, looking for Mr. Helton. Mr. Hatch is the rationalizing man at his most perplexing. He is the arm, the self-appointed arm, of justice, common law, and formal statutes. He has come to get Mr. Helton, because Mr. Helton is a murderer and an escaped lunatic, a dangerous man, carrying a reward for his apprehension. The apprehender, though, as Glenway Wescott has said eloquently in his own way in *Images of Truth*, is the criminal, rather than Mr. Helton, because the lawful man's crime is a crime against all of humanity, though he has every sanction on his side.

But at the center of the story is that briefly fortunate man, Mr. Thompson, whose farm has been pulled together so miraculously and set running: he murders the intruder, or at least axes him down in the stress of a moment, is brought to trial, and exonerated, and then cannot get anyone to believe that he actually was guiltless. He has no way to relax his efforts to rationalize the inescapable ambiguity of his own conduct, and he detects the heartless rationalizing of others going on, always directed against him. Deep in their minds even his wife and his sons have doubts about him, he has protested so much; and he shoots himself.

The question is, was his use of the axe a justifiable défense of Mr. Helton? or a defense of his own personal interest in retaining Mr. Helton? There is no answer. The worst of answers are those freely and confidently offered when there is none.

For "Noon Wine" Miss Porter put together some twenty years later an account of what had originally started the story off in her imagination. What she says is of interest not simply for its bearing on "Noon Wine" but rather more, I think, for its pertinence to all writing, her own and everyone's. Her recollections appeared first in the *Yale Review* in 1956, after her essays had already been collected in *The Days Before*, but the article has appeared again in Brooks and Warren, *Understanding Fiction*. The part that concerns me most is the following:

I do know why I remembered. . . .

Why, that is to say, she remembered a shotgun blast, a scream, a nervous horse, a little tune.

I do know why I remembered. . . . and why in my memory they slowly took on their separate lives in a story. It is because there radiated from each one of those glimpses of strangers some element, some quality that arrested my attention at a vital moment in my own growth, and caused me, a child, to stop short and look outward, away from myself; to look at another human being with that attention and wonder and speculation which ordinarily, and very naturally, a child lavishes only on himself.

To look at another human being, really to do so, is a fairly rare occurrence, but it is worth it, frightening though the shock of it may sometimes be.

Using the norms of prose fiction Katherine Anne Porter can be as graphic in her portraiture of folly as were the collaborators in the many editions and translations of Sebastian Brant's *Das Narrenschiff* [Ship of Fools] (1494), and the artists who made the jostling, crowded woodcuts to illustrate them, and as forceful as the Dante-Doré pages of the *Inferno*, or the Erasmus-More-Holbein *Praise of Folly*. Hers is a healthy, corrosive point of view. Like the imagination of those others, all of whom she learned to know well early in her life, hers has implicit in it its impenetrable shadows and blinding shimmers.

Her point of view has provoked dissension, as I said at first. William L. Nance, in a long and tediously involved book, stands as spokesman for the not uncommon charge that Miss Porter's work follows a pattern which "is a completely negative one and the view of life which corresponds to it is one of unrelieved darkness." This study assumes that developments since the passing of Modernism make the austerities of Miss Porter particularly untenable. The idea seems to be that a renewal of faith in generous, loving, optimistic, religious "certainties" has become the rule among good minds during the last decade or two. And it may be so. But the charges against Miss Porter sound very much like a repetition of the charges against Thomas Hardy, and many another; well-intentioned perhaps, but notably imperceptive.

Anyhow, let's consider *Ship of Fools*. I dislike the thought of stressing "positive" elements in this big, naked, colossal novel; I have no confidence in the distinction between positive and negative as the terms are presently used; but since the range of the book puts comprehensive treatment out of reach, I'll try to count off a few of its accomplishments; which of course in my mind are not negative things. As for its overall effect, it will not reveal itself at a glance. The motion picture conveys a good impression, and is an exceptional film, but it simplifies. The real thing asks the reader to give it a fair share of his reading time.

The events take place in the deceptively slow stages of a very long voyage, complete with the crazed surfaces of embarkation and disembarkation, and the long glazed interval in between. The motion of the book is unique. Each of Miss Porter's short stories has characteristically a motion of its own, an oral and visual progression appropriate to the telling in each case of the story as a straight story. *Ship of Fools* is a weaving, a tapestry, a book of woodcuts, a Dance of Death, or it may be of Life.

There are many people in it, and like the little knots of people in the short stories they are hardly to be labelled *good*. They have one failing in common. They are determined to extort acts of love from their fellow creatures, whether they are worthy themselves to be recipients of such acts or not. With this natural rapacity for love, in all senses of the term, they present themselves hopefully to others, while watching almost exclusively for signs of the acceptance or rejection of their hopes.

The well-to-do are "rather self-absorbed," as Mrs. Treadwell observes about David, while she herself induces in herself her own self-absorbed dreams of days of wine and roses in Paris, in what is transparently both a criticism and a parody of a page in Scott Fitzgerald. The poorer passengers, among them the zarzuela dancers, are vicious in their demands on others; but perhaps no more so in the case of the dancers than their business as prostitutes and pimps demands, and as Dr. Schumann remarks the latter have at least some arts as entertainers that more or less made amends for their evil ways. The really poor human cargo below decks has its saints, but on the whole it remains anonymous, sunk in poverty.

Human beings, these fare-paying passengers, human to a fault. At one place Wilhelm Freytag, being buffeted like everyone else on the ship against everyone else, indulges himself in impatience with human nature.

He had discovered . . . about most persons that their abstractions and generalizations, their Rage for Justice or Hatred of

Tyranny or whatever, too often disguised a bitter personal grudge of some sort far removed from the topic apparently under discussion.

But that sage observation of Freytag's induces also the following sad commentary:

He did not once include himself in it.

And yet it is always possible that the rationalizing man coming so close to other rationalizing men, may begin one day to suspect his abstractions and generalizations and to be consequently just a little bit more thoughtful about parading them. There is always the possibility of seeing things somewhat afresh, without predatory interests, like catching sight of the naked feet of the Indian nursemaid under the skirt of her elaborate traveling dress.

And this *Ship of Fools* is full of surprises. These human beings have so many astonishing capacities, so many comical aspects, so much dogged persistence in their natures, that they deserve, in this long-range view of them, to be taken with something less than deadly seriousness. It must be pleasantly significant that Ampara and Pepe, whore and pimp though they are, love each other and make love with all of the slow fury and authenticity that a growing boy could dream of; and not only they, but Herr Professor and Frau Hutten in their grief over events that exceeded their powers of comprehension.

It is both pleasant and gently significant that Herr Rieber, when he tries negotiating with the fat purser for a new cabin mate, has to contend with all of the malice and unction of a German ship's officer, only to be given his choice between retaining his present companion, whose Jewish connections offend him, or taking in with him the violent Swede who, although Nordic, threatens to do him violence on the least provocation.

There is a sequence of matchless little scenes in which the zarzuela dancers are selling tickets to their fiesta and lottery, which is a transparent fraud, and the passengers are seeking, each in his own way, to protect themselves. One exchange I think is worth setting down in detail, because it runs counter to the other exchanges and exhibits quite vividly the counter-theme that has continued through Miss Porter's work from first to last.

Manola bowed to little Señora Ortega, bent over her deck chair offering tickets and a shattering fire of explanations. The Indian nurse, sitting near holding the baby, glanced quickly at the tickets and away again, face calm, eyelids lowered. She could not read words, but she could smell a chance-game at a great distance, she knew numbers when she saw them, and bought a fraction of every lottery that came along, because she knew one more thing very well: for her kind, born on the straw mat, barefoot from dirt floor to grave, there was only one hope of fortune—to hit the lucky number, just once! Her dead mother often spoke to her anxiously in dreams: "Nicolasa, my child, listen now to me carefully—listen, do you hear me, Nicolasa? I am about to give you the winning number for the next lottery. Buy the whole ticket, look until you find the seller who has it. He is in Cinco de Mayo street. His name is . . ." and always as she began to recite his name, the number, the serial, all, her words would run together, her face grow dim, her voice die away, and Nicolasa, waking in fright, would hear herself calling out, "Oh wait, Mother! Don't go . . . tell me, tell me!" Señora Ortega smiled at the expression on Nicolasa's face. She knew it well, and what it meant. She bought the two tickets from Manola and gave them without a word to the Indian girl, who would have kissed Señora Ortega's hand if she had not instantly taken it back.

And then sometimes the sudden revelation of some rare and surprising polarity in life itself shakes the ship and allows the voyagers for a moment to stand apart from themselves and take a new look out over the horizon. Once, on the occasion of the sea-burial of the selfless little man Echegaray, it was the sight of three whales—"three enormous whales, seeming to swim almost out of the water, flashing white silver in the sunlight, . . . going south—not one person could take his eyes from the beautiful spectacle until it was over, and their minds were cleansed of death and violence." At another time it was the discovery of the water-bearers of Tenerife, beautiful tall girls running with water-containers on their heads—these were creatures too who took them out of themselves and set their minds to work on a conception of a circumstance in which bearers of burdens would be lovely, active, and chaste. And then, at the end of the voyage, it was the granite spine of Spain: on that beautiful coast, "after the solid promontory of rock, a great table rising out of the sea."

Coming at last under the lee of the ancient rock which is Europe, one passenger, at least one, is able to reconstruct his awareness of another. David creates a truer Jenny for himself; he still has to rely on "the stray stuffs of his own desire"; but his old habitual views and impressions and feelings about her, and about himself, are gone. David and Jenny do improve, once they have arrived, after painful course, at knowing each other a little better.

I would like to think that the days and years in Mexico nurtured Miss Porter's awareness of the peculiar dispositions of world-travelers who find themselves hung up for the moment in a slow boat. But I don't know. Life in Denver or New York, or Texas or Germany or Paris, affords opportunity enough for noticing how passengers behave. Still the absolutely clear definition of so many quick glances at faces and at gestures, and inward at the motions of minds and feelings, seems to come from the oblique angle of some older native point of view, looking with intense interest and some amusement at strangers rushing by.

The Way to Read *Gatsby*

RICHARD FOSTER

Because it is such a perfect critic's piece—compact, complex, and propertied with symbols—*The Great Gatsby* has been one of the most written about classics of modern fiction in English. It has also been, surely, one of the most peaceably written about. Practically to a man the critics have praised its "form," by which they have chiefly meant the control, distancing, and complication which Fitzgerald gives to the portrait of Gatsby through his subtle use of intelligent, detached, principled, skeptical and ironic, but humanely compassionate Nick Carraway as narrator. A few years back Robert W. Stallman disturbed the peace somewhat by taking the view that Nick is a sentimental hypocrite and moral paralytic whose presence as narrator has the effect of radically heightening, through contrast, the shimmer of Gatsby's heroic radiance. Frederick J. Hoffman, speaking for established critical opinion, peremptorily dismissed Stallman's reading as "an exaggerated and often incorrect interpretation." A more recent critic, also unable to ignore the obtrusive evidence of Nick's gravely flawed conscience and spirit, saved himself from a like censure by deciding that, after all, the novel is an intellectual and formal failure and its creator soft-headed.[1]

This last judgment, though attached to a shrewd enough analysis of Nick Carraway, is not very much more difficult to put aside than was Eliot's devaluation of Milton or Ransom's of Shakespeare. But it nevertheless suggests, as does Stallman's reinterpretation, that the praise accorded *Gatsby* by a whole generation of critics may have been based on a mistaken, or at least distorted, perception of its object. If so, Nick Carraway seems to have been the cause of the trouble. For as exemplars of a neoclassical and "formalist" age of criticism, the critics seem to have found it both right and natural to identify their own style of moral intelligence with that of neoclassical Nick. And perhaps, therefore, the style of their regard for the novel—like Nick's of its hero—has cheated it of its warranted full measure of recognition as a deft masterpiece of affirmative romantic imagination.

My aim is to suggest here a better way of reading *The Great Gatsby*, a way of reading it that will redeem the novel —and along with it one of its most astute commentators, Mr. Stallman—from the prejudices and errors of most of its critics. And a corrective beginning can be made by renouncing, for the moment, Conrad and James as providers of relevant models for comparison, and turning instead to a book which, in its subtle interplay of form and meaning, *Gatsby* far more acutely resembles than any of theirs: Ford Madox Ford's *The Good Soldier*.

Both *The Good Soldier* and *The Great Gatsby* deal with contradictions present in a romantic figure, certain troubling discrepancies between appearance and reality which that figure reveals under critical scrutiny. And both books similarly complicate the investigative adventure by conveying it through the viewpoint of a narrator-commentator who is as ambiguous and apparently dichotomous in his own way as is the object of his attention. In both books on ironic narrator with definite but repressed understrains of sentiment and idealism contemplates the prospect of an ingenuous hero whose nobility is qualified by absurdity and dishonesty. The narrative form of both books thus suggests the epistemological and moral questions which constitute a large share of their themes: What is real? What is true? And in neither book can the answers to these questions be much more than "distilled," as essences of implication, from an examination of the vis à vis placement of narrator and hero. Because we see Gatsby and the world he inhabits only through Nick's eyes, an objective understanding of Nick is vital to our understanding of Gatsby and the moral meaning of his story. And Nick, as I shall argue, is not quite what he takes himself to be, nor what most commentators on the novel, agreeably seeing him as he sees himself, have taken him to be.

Nick sees the world, twentieth-century America, as a moral and spiritual wasteland, its departed god suggestively memorialized in the sightless presiding eyes of the absent Dr. Eckleburg's sign. He sees Gatsby as an Apollo or Prometheus, the type of the hero or god reincarnate, who transforms, for a brief term, not only himself but the world around him before he becomes the half-absurd, half-tragic victim of history's inevitably reasserted laws. To Nick, Gatsby is a beautiful if fragile redeemer of modern secularist materialism, creating out of that very substance quite another reality. Beauty and meaning are born where Gatsby casts his glance. A world gathers round him, becomes peopled, and for a while lives according to the laws of his vision —the "reality" created by the nearly superhuman force of his desire, his will, his imagination.

For Nick, Gatsby's coming enlightens with a certain splendor and nobility the wasteland nothingness of the present surveyed by the blind eyes of Dr. Eckleburg. Gatsby has that rare and magically creative endowment of personality first isolated and defined as "radiance" in *This Side of Paradise*. And throughout the novel Nick hungrily drinks in this "radiance" of Gatsby's as if it were rich spiritual nourishment. "I am the son of some wealthy people in the Middle West," this "son of God" tells the skeptical but magnetized Nick Carraway:

I was brought up in America but educated at Oxford, because all my ancestors have been educated there for many years. It is a family tradition. . . . My family all died and I came into a good deal of money. . . . After that I lived like a young rajah in all the capitals of Europe . . . trying to forget something very sad that happened to me long ago. . . . Then came the war, old sport. It was a great relief, and I tried very hard to die. . . . In the Argonne forest I took two machine-gun detachments so far forward that there was a half mile gap on either side of us where the infantry couldn't advance. . . . I was promoted to be a major, and every Allied government gave me a decoration—even Montenegro, little Montenegro down on the Adriatic Sea!

And Gatsby had begun this initial recital to Nick, who is already on the way to becoming his apostle and chronicler, by vowing, "I'll tell you God's truth."

If Gatsby is the bright Phoebus of redemptive vision, Tom Buchanan, Gatsby's opposite, and therefore his enemy, is prince of the "real" world, a world beyond redemption. He is described thus by Nick:

He was a sturdy straw-haired man of thirty with a rather hard mouth and a supercilious manner. Two shining arrogant eyes had established dominance over his face and gave him the appearance of always leaning aggressively forward. Not even the effeminate swank of his riding clothes could hide the enormous power of that body—he seemed to fill those glistening boots until he strained the top lacing, and you could see a great pack of muscle shifting when his shoulder moved under his thin coat. It was a body capable of enormous leverage—a cruel body.

He is as brutal as Gatsby is gentle, as vulgarly authentic as Gatsby is beautifully "absurd." He is one of Fitzgerald's "rich," a physically emphatic equivalent of another of Fitzgerald's rich boys, Anson Hunter, blighted hero of "The Rich Boy" (1926), who, without love, insight, or humility, wields, like Tom Buchanan, the power of life and death over those within his sphere. Because they are born to the possession of the enormous power conferred by money, there is no distance between the rich boys and the desirable things of the world they live in. They do not, like Gatsby, make images to live by because they cannot know what it is to dream, to strive, to believe, even to love. They don't have to do any of these things, and so they do not understand them. Creatures combining "fractiousness" and "paternal contempt," as Nick says of Tom, they grow into tyrants without ceasing basically to be children. They cannot grow because they cannot know what it is either to dream or to fail. And so they can only exist as personified forces of the actual world. "Careless people," as Nick says of Tom and Daisy near the end of the novel, they are as impersonal and ineluctable as nature itself: "They smashed up things and creatures and then retreated back into their money or their vast carelessness, or whatever it was that kept them together, and let other people clean up the mess they had made."

This hardest lesson yielded up by Nick's questing pilgrimage in the east—that the dream-led hero is doomed to destruction by the reductive laws of the reality that he would transform and transcend—is also the last. Gatsby's vision, the "form" of his life's enterprise, disintegrates at last before a concatenation of the "real" world's reflexive energies; the Buchanans and their meaning persist and prevail; and Nick turns back to the prudential stabilities of his Middle West. As the novel's narrative form itself implies, though Nick's perception and understanding have been augmented and changed by his experience, Nick himself has not. Back home again, the style of his life will return to essentially what it had been before his removal to the East. He has seen Gatsby, appraised him, valued him, witnessed his cause and been touched, moved, exalted by the prospect of his tragic destiny. Like Gatsby himself, he has come into the possession of a new vision. But unlike Gatsby he has not been possessed by it. He does not, as he says Gatsby does, become born anew from some "Platonic conception of himself" derived from his vision of Gatsby. To discern how and why this is so—to adjudicate and interpret the radical opposition of Gatsby and Nick in terms of the polarities of value and motive that form the conflicts of *The Great Gatsby*—is to uncover meanings in the novel which considerably complicate and deepen those more available ones that have already been discussed.

At the beginning of *The Great Gatsby*, Nick Carraway implicitly certifies himself in his role as interpreter-narrator by declaring his cultivation of the virtue of tolerance: "I'm inclined to reserve all judgments, a habit that has opened up many curious natures to me and also made me the victim of not a few veteran bores." "Reserving judgments," he says, as if to explain the *virtus* of his virtue, "is a matter of infinite hope." And yet he is no mere transparency, but rather a continual and forceful judgmental voice throughout the novel —a voice judging, for example, Daisy. Nick reflects on her chic cynicism about the modern age and her plight in it, a role which she plays for him on his first visit to East Egg: "It made me uneasy, as though the whole evening had been a trick of some sort to exact a contributory emotion from me."

At Gatsby's party Daisy observes a movie star whose hovering and attentive director finally kisses her on the cheek. " 'I like her,' said Daisy, 'I think she's lovely.' " Nick comments, offering no grounds for his complaint,

But the rest offended her—and inarguably, because it wasn't a gesture but an emotion. She was appalled by West Egg, this unprecedented "place" that Broadway had begotten upon a Long Island fishing village—appalled by its raw vigor that chafed under the old euphemisms and by the too obtrusive fate that herded its inhabitants along a short-cut from nothing to nothing.

And later, before the fateful excursion to New York, Nick's gratuitous fragment of a remark about Daisy, "She's got an indiscreet voice . . . It's full of—" is suddenly defined as compulsive, harsh, rancorous, by Gatsby's ingenuous statement of spontaneously perceived fact: "Her voice is full of money." "They're a rotten crowd," Nick shouts back across the lawn to Gatsby, who has finally become the victim of both disillusion and "reality," "You're worth the whole damn bunch put together." This summary judgment, strong, final, and unmistakably inclusive even of Daisy, the ideal object or form of Gatsby's own vision, is remarkable not only because of its breadth but also because it is one of the rare moments in which Nick expresses his feelings directly and nakedly, without any veil or coloration of irony.

Irony is the technique of Nick Carraway's detachment. It is simultaneously a protective barrier he sets between himself and "life" and a kind of pseudo weaponry of selection and judgment that he fires off, from a safe distance, at the scene passing before him. As Gatsby's vision is romantic and ingenuous to the point of absurdity, Nick's vision is ironic and reductive to the point of sentimentality. The two extremes nearly meet on the battlegrounds of the War—Gatsby trying hard to die but in spite of himself falling into heroism, Nick so enjoying the "counter-raid" to "that delayed Teutonic migration known as the Great War" that he comes back home "restless." As readers of Hemingway know, the aria of overstatement and the grunt of understatement are nearly the same voice when the subject is ego rather than truth. An application of something like the same principle to Nick's opening statements of his "tolerance," especially in the light of his impressively "judgey" application of nearly universal irony throughout the rest of the book, yields similar second thoughts. "Whenever you feel like criticizing any one," Nick's father had advised him in youth, "just remember that all the people in this world haven't had the advantages that you've had." The advice is in itself outrageously smug, and of course Nick ironizes about "boasting" of a tolerance based on so "snobbish" a principle. And yet his father's imperative *is* a fair statement of the nature and degree of Nick's tolerance and of the principle that explains his mind and temperament. Nick's putting it in range of his irony is not, therefore, a disclaimer, but rather a way of distancing it and defending it, and himself as its exponent. The irony is the mark of its validation.

Opposite as they are in certain very obvious ways—mostly in the area of self-knowledge—there is a striking moral similarity between Nick Carraway and Tom Buchanan, especially when one views the two in comparison with Gatsby. The similarity is not easy to name definitively, but it has to do with dreaming and feeling. Tom, the rich boy born to the power of wealth, cannot learn the meaning of aspiration nor know what it is to "dream" as Gatsby does. As Nick says in his corrosively "understanding" manner, Tom is "a national figure in a way, one of those men who reach such an acute limited excellence at twenty-one that everything afterwards savors of anticlimax." He is less human, as a consequence, than he should be. He has been brutalized by the luck of his birth. But so, in another way, has Nick. For Nick is also one of the "very rich," though in another sense. As Tom has been born to riches, Nick has been born, as he himself knows and confesses, to moral certainty. Tom is one of the powerful, Nick one of the righteous. And though both can know the frustration of the child who is denied, neither can know what it is to undertake the hazardous remaking of life in the lineaments of some dream. This is why dangerous Tom fears and hates Gatsby, while ironic Nick eyes him with the timorous passion of the fan-club cultist. And the paradox is completed by the fact that innocent, visionary, heroic Gatsby is up to his eyebrows, as Tom and Nick are not, in the murderous and corrupting give-and-take of "the world."

Gatsby is *alive*, as Nick and Tom are not. But one distinction between Nick and Tom on this ground is of course that Nick knows it and Tom does not. "Almost any exhibition of complete self-sufficiency," Nick reflects, recalling Jordan Baker's perfectly laconic detachment at his first meeting with her, "draws a stunned tribute from me."

Fitzgerald did not need Jordan Baker as a major character for any other reason than to amplify the character of his narrator. And since there was ample precedent in the work of Joseph Conrad, the serious novelist he revered most, for the use of a wise, objective, speculative interpreter-narrator wholly severed from the dramatic consequences of his subject matter, one can only conclude that because Fitzgerald handled his narrator so differently he had very special dramatic and therefore thematic functions in mind for him. Jordan, as an ironic mirror to Nick, is perhaps the chief means of registering those functions. She is at once "like" Nick, detached and ironic, and yet unlike him: she has style (she is "haughty" in her detachment), she is in the world (a golf champion), and she is willing, though apparently only after much prior rumination, to invest her emotions in love of someone she thinks is like herself ("I hate careless people," she says to Nick. "That's why I like you.") Nick had become interested in Jordan in a certain cool way ("flattered to go places with her"), then it turned into something more: "I wasn't actually in love, but I felt a sort of tender curiosity." *Curiosity*—the most characteristic, and very nearly the intensest, relationship for Nick to establish *re* another human being—leads to revelations. He finds the rotten spot in Jordan's armor: "dishonesty." (Birds of a feather . . .) But when Jordan makes her understated declaration of commitment to him, Nick's built-in mechanism of inherited integrity goes into operation. He remembers that all the while Jordan has been in his eye and on his mind as the object of his "curiosity" he has been writing weekly letters signed "Love, Nick" to a "vague understanding" back home whom he feels he must break with before he can be free for Jordan. Says Nick of himself at this juncture, whether or not ironically, "Every one suspects himself of at least one of the cardinal virtues, and this is mine: I am one of the few honest people that I have ever known."

After the series of disasters that culminate in Gatsby's murder Nick feels that he must go home, that he must turn away from all those aspects of the terrible East that have brought about this tragic dissolution. He goes to see Jordan, and with her usual style she informs him "without comment" that she is engaged to someone else. But before he departs she challenges him:

> "It was careless of me to make such a wrong guess. I thought you were rather an honest, straightforward person. I thought it was your secret pride."
> "I'm thirty," I said. "I'm five years too old to lie to myself and call it honor."
> She didn't answer. Angry, and half in love with her, and tremendously sorry, I turned away.

Jordan, of course, has here touched one of Nick's own rotten spots just as Nick originally searched out and finally found hers, and his sentimental mask of feeling at the end of this exchange does not quite suffice to obscure the significance of her discovery and the jolt he suffers when she names it without qualm: dishonesty. The word goes to many targets, becomes the key to many hints that have lain hidden from the beginning beneath Nick's role and mask.

Nick the scorner of artifice in others is all artifice himself. When things become too real for this detached epicure of the flights and failures of others, specifically when the currents of actual life threaten to envelop him, Nick draws back. He prefers the role of onlooker, and he even enjoys watching himself play it. Just before the fateful return from New York with Tom and Jordan, Nick remembers that it is his birthday: "I was thirty. Before me stretched the portentous menacing road of a new decade." Characteristically, Nick turns away from "reality"—from Tom's voice "exulting and laughing," "the foreign clamor on the sidewalk," "the tumult of the elevated overhead"—in order to nurture images of his own pathos:

Human sympathy has its limits, and we were content to let all their tragic arguments fade with the city lights behind. Thirty—the promise of a decade of loneliness, a thinning briefcase of enthusiasms, thinning hair. But there was Jordan beside me, who, unlike Daisy, was too wise ever to carry well-forgotten dreams from age to age.

Nick is wrong about Jordan, who, through an equally mistaken conception of what *he* is, has chosen him. When Gatsby is overtaken by disaster and Nick, feeling that he can take no more of reality, decides to go home, it is significant that he also decides to leave Jordan behind. This decision and Jordan's already cited judgment of it, quite clearly places Jordan among the living. And of course it also places Nick—but rather differently.

Nick is one of life's voyeurs, his gaze trained on the clash between the world's matter and power and "the dream," and on the human figures who bring these antithetical constituents of reality to personifying human focus. He identifies with both sides of the conflict, in a sense, projecting his unfulfilled desires into Gatsby, his unpurged guilts into Daisy, Tom, Jordan, "the world." When he cries out to Gatsby, "You're worth the whole damn bunch put together," he is addressing in part a sentimental image of himself as lonely hero. There is at times a crazy confusion in his responses ("If personality is an unbroken series of successful gestures, then there was something gorgeous about him"), crazy because he is writing a kind of paean to Gatsby, and "gestures" in others, Daisy for example, are despicable for their "insincerity." But the feeling for Gatsby and his meaning continues to come across, and sometimes it even breaks through into the words that it warrants: "It was an extraordinary gift for hope, a romantic readiness such as I have never found in any other person and which it is not likely I shall ever find again." It is easy to see why Nick had no love left—no *real* love—for Jordan Baker. Gatsby's "radiance" had touched Nick's "curiosity" and turned it into love; when Gatsby is destroyed by the accidents of reality, Nick's sense of life turns into nausea and suffocation—horror: "it is what preyed on Gatsby, what foul dust floated in the wake of his dreams that temporarily closed out my interest in the abortive sorrows and short-winded elations of men."

But "interest" is very nearly all that his feeling had ever really amounted to, and one imagines that it will indeed be only "temporarily" suspended—a more or less successful gesture of retreat indicating wounded sensibility—and that this Jacques, this sentimental Thersites, will be back at his post again before long viewing the passing parade. Yes, interest is very nearly all, but not quite all. There is something else. A memory . . . a memory that wants to stir into life as Nick remembers listening to Gatsby's narrative of his discovery of Daisy and his choosing her in the moment of the incarnation kiss:

I was reminded of something—an elusive rhythm, a fragment of lost words, that I had heard somewhere a long time ago. For a moment a phrase tried to take shape in my mouth and my lips parted like a dumb man's, as though there was more struggling upon them than a wisp of startled air. But they made no sound, and what I had almost remembered was uncommunicable for-ever.

What Nick cannot quite remember, what he has perhaps either killed in himself or never had the courage to begin to know, is what Dexter Green, in "Winter Dreams" (1922), has known once—"the moment" of love, life, being, fully and intensely realized, and also the aftermath knowledge of its loss, which remains as the measure of having lived, the mark of one's achieved humanity:

He pushed the palms of his hands into his eyes and tried to bring up a picture of the waters lapping on Sherry Island and the moonlit veranda, and gingham on the golf-links and the dry sun and the gold color of her neck's soft down. And her mouth damp to his kisses and her eyes plaintive with melancholy and her freshness like new fine linen in the morning. Why, these things were no longer in the world! They had existed and they existed no longer.

For the first time in years the tears were streaming down his face. But they were for himself now. He did not care about mouth and eyes and moving hands. He wanted to care, and he could not care. For he had gone away and he could never go back any more. The gates were closed, the sun was gone down, and there was no beauty but the gray beauty of steel that withstands all time. Even the grief he could have borne was left behind in the country of illusion, of youth, of the richness of life, where his winter dreams had flourished.

It would be a mistake to understand Nick Carraway simply as a more knowing, more self-possessed, more "mature" Dexter Green, because to do so would be to misunderstand, by extension, the crucial *qualitative* distinction that Fitzgerald is at pains to render fully in *The Great Gatsby*. There are ampler dimensions in life available to Gatsby, and more modestly to Dexter Green, that Nick Carraway can know nothing about—as suggested in the passage on his reaction to the incarnation kiss—or know only in the distorted shadow forms presented to his deprived perspective of skeptical detachment and defensive moralism. Apropos of Fitzgerald's excitement at reading Maurois' *Ariel* as he was approaching the completion of *The Great Gatsby*, he wrote to Maxwell Perkins in June of 1924, "Shelley was a God to me once. What a good man he is compared to that colossal egotist Browning!" Gatsby is the Shelley of his world, and Nick Carraway, speaking relatively, is its Browning. Gatsby lives, and Nick watches, transmuting the sustenance he takes therefrom into a complex, pseudo-moral system of justifications for his vicarious existence. Nick can be best understood, then, as an extension of Anthony Patch. Both Anthony and Nick are weak and both are "egotist"; and both are moral failures because they are human, which is to say "emotional," failures. But unlike Anthony, Nick survives because he has learned the trick of turning his negatives into ostensible positives.

As the materialist, the illusionist, and the moralist, or however else one might appropriately name them and indicate their relationships to each other, Tom, Gatsby, and Nick together add up to a paradigm of the permanent tendencies, drives, and tensions, the universal "laws," of human temperament operative in any time or place. But the strong local and historical feeling of *The Great Gatsby* as a novel—the sense throughout it that the world has got itself into a grim historical *cul de sac*, that values are "dead," and so on—invites an understanding of these characters' roles, and the "laws" of human thought and feeling suggested by them, in the historical perspective as well. Viewed against the background *Angst* characterizing the historically predicated "modern world," Nick seems to take on the special significance of having changed, *as a type*, under the effects of history, while his compeers, as types, have not. His moral essence shows signs of permutations, theirs do not. Gatsby is Hotspur reborn as a modern and he flourishes and falls in this world much as he did in that other where "honor" was a reality. And Tom is an arrogant, as truculent, as "careless," and even though he does not go under, is as pitifully blind and vulnerable, as Shakespeare's Caesar. But Nick, whom we recognize as the contemplative man, the knower and thinker, is no Brutus, certainly no Hamlet. He could not be either one of them in this world and yet survive to function as the Jacques-Thersites commentator on the bitterly comic tragedy of absurdities that history has concocted for his witness.

Though Fitzgerald admitted to having learned much from the art of Joseph Conrad, the novelist he admired above all others, Nick is no Conradian narrator, above all no Marlow. At their worst Conrad's narrators are simple, never bad, nor even weak. They were born and bred in reverence of the old heroic virtues, and it is this standard of human value that they bring to bear on the stories they tell and interpret to us. Nick is very different, not only because he never lived the life of action that Marlow did, but because he was formed by that "modern" world that had only begun to be born when Marlow disappeared. Furthermore, Nick's return to the West at the end of the novel is quite obviously a very different thing from the moral nobility of Jim's return, in

Lord Jim, to the "destructive element" of life that he had once fled, or Isabel's return to face the grim music of marriage to Osmond in James' *Portrait of a Lady*. But it is not, after all, so very different from Lambert Strether's ostensibly renunciatory return from Europe and the joys and challenges of "life" to Woollett, Massachusetts and the justice of Mrs. Newsome in *The Ambassadors*. And because it is not, it tends to expose, in its incisive portrayal of the self-camouflaging weaknesses and hypocrisies of the Carraway-Strether type, the basic sentimentality of that celebrated—and, incidentally, hyperironic—work of James. Prufrock is Strether in parody. And Carraway is Prufrock, in turn, taken seriously, given his due as well as his knocks, in that he is shown possessing in spite of his negativeness, a disturbing effectiveness. Nick Carraway is the modern man of integrity; and Fitzgerald's characterization of him as subtly corrupt and potentially corrupting in his relations with the unlucky people he observes constitutes a shrewd and original comment on the new laws of consequence that make the modern world modern. The skill with which Nick masks chronic fear and neurotic curiosity as tenderness of feeling and piercing intelligence is nearly that of a poet. It is a skill largely of words. And in this novel words are the life-medium of the impotent man.

Nick's weavings of words compose and interpret the most part of the moral reality confronting our judgment and understanding as we read *The Great Gatsby*. And sometimes, as in those last magnificent paragraphs about the meaning of America, the end of history, and the deathlessness of man's tragic appetite for wonder, he is a very great and true poet indeed. But he is also suggestively placed as a character in relation to other characters within the action whose narration his sensibility controls, encompasses, and so effectively shades and highlights. He has *his* author, too, that is to say; and he cannot, as Ford's Dowell could not, entirely becloud the fact that he is an object within the purview of yet another intelligence. Tested by the norms of that intelligence, Nick's moral vision is at best of an uncertain purity, and his harsh, poignant, gross, beautiful, and always engaging recreations of it in words, are a kind of siren song whose seductions are quite clearly discerned and definitely to be resisted. Nick Carraway's moralism is insistently negative. There is nothing one can "do" with his counsel except turn from life, retreat, grieve, and perhaps pine away listening to the beautiful music of his statement of his vision, and like Keats, drunk with the music of his nightingale, die rapturously at last into oblivion.

But even Nick's own wishful vision of beautiful futility recognizes the continual phoenix-rebirth of dream and aspiration as the fountainhead of human history. It was Amory Blaine, the hero of Fitzgerald's first novel, who discovered and accepted the moral philosophy that one must, after defeat and failure, pick up and go on to "the next thing." Putting behind him Nick Carraway's rendering of a blind-end world in *The Great Gatsby*, and taking with him that part of it which has value as usable human truth, Fitzgerald went on, as an artist, to the "next thing" in *Tender Is the Night*, which is the story of a man who, with much fuller knowledge of the inexorable laws of reality than innocent Gatsby had, nevertheless pitted his character, his integrity, his personal vision and energy, flawed and imperfect as they were, against the futility and despair that he knew were the ruling truths of his world.

Mark Twain Among the Malefactors

LEWIS LEARY

Samuel Clemens had a cold when he landed in New York on September 7, 1893, hurrying home from Europe to see what could be done in this panic year about his investments in the Paige typesetting machine and in his publishing company which floundered now in—he thought—the incompetent hands of an incompetent nephew. To cure the cold, he drank "almost a whole bottle" of whiskey, went warmly to bed, and got up the next morning, he boasted to his daughter, "perfectly well." But his throat was a constant trouble to him— even giving up smoking every night did not cure it; so he was acquainted perforce, and gladly, with Dr. Clarence C. Rice, a jovial fellow-member of the Players Club, and a specialist in such matters who did or would cure the throats of other celebrities, like Edwin Booth, Enrico Caruso, and Lillian Russell. He was "a physician of great reputation," thought Clemens, "and one of the choicest human beings in the world."

He stayed with Dr. Rice at his home at 123 East 19th Street during his first weeks in New York, while he scurried about on Wall Street and among the banks, trying desperately to raise money for his ailing enterprises. None was to be had, not "at any rate of interest whatever, or upon any security, or by *anybody*." Seeing his friend's distress, Dr. Rice came to his rescue. He had another patient who was wealthy ("a rich friend of his who was an admirer of mine," Clemens later explained), and he told him of the straits Mark Twain was in, and then he introduced him to the rich friend, and neither Samuel Clemens nor Mark Twain was ever quite the same again.

The rich friend was Henry Huttleston Rogers, and he and Clemens hit it off splendidly, and at once.[1] They were two of a kind, and they even looked alike. Each had been a poor boy; each had risen in the true American tradition; each was now, in his own right, famous. Rogers was of New England background, and he had known the oil fields of Pennsylvania much as Clemens had known the silver fields of Nevada and the gold fields of California, and now, in 1893, he was executive head of the gigantic Standard Oil Company, known with John D. and William Rockefeller, John D. Archbold, and Henry M. Flagler as one of the more wealthy and most ruthless men of his time. "Hell-hound Rogers," he was called, a pirate and a butcher, a malefactor of great wealth. "No punishable offense," said the New York *Times*, had ever been formally proved against him, but his "share in the unfair and abhorrent methods of Standard Oil was so considerable that he ought therefore to have suffered increasing torments of remorse; and undoubtedly he did not so suffer."

Rogers's Midas touch in speculation was one which Colonel Sellers, or Samuel Clemens, might well envy. The capitalist who manipulated monopolies in oil and copper and railroads seemed not unlike the Boss from the Hartford firearms shop who in *The Connecticut Yankee* with equal bravado and native skill, and with some explosive help from gunpowder, bested Merlin and routed the enemies of King Arthur. How close and warm and rakish became the friendship between these two; they were cronies in every best sense. Rogers was the kind of man Clemens most admired—bold, swashbuckling, with a sense of humor, and with millions on millions of dollars: "He is not only the best friend I have ever had, but is the best man I have known." And yet there was something Faustian also about their relationship.

Whatever his public image, Rogers was in private, among his friends and in his family, the kindliest of men, a good companion, quietly witty, and warmly responsive. He loved good stories, and told them well, and he loved the theater; he had even a few years earlier published a volume of homely verse—but he never said much about that. Among friends, he was a man's man, who played poker and billiards, liked boxing matches and fast racing yachts (and bought himself one that could outrun even Pierpont Morgan's famed *Corsair*). He was a gruff and affectionate companion, and he and Clemens greeted each other with affectionate, unprintable insults when they met, swapping yarns and schemes for getting Mark Twain out of financial troubles. Clemens envied his new friend, the way he got things done—"no grass grew under his feet"—and the way he manipulated people (like Tom Sawyer, only ever so much more profitably). He liked to lounge in Rogers's office at 26 Broadway, listening entranced to the manipulations of high finance. He dreamed sometimes that he might manipulate that way.

But even Rogers's magic touch and helpful money could not immediately save Clemens. When the publishing company went bankrupt and the typesetting machine proved impractical, debts mounted to over two hundred thousand dollars. Could they be paid, and Clemens approaching sixty? Rogers thought that they could and should be. Clemens was not sure on either count; he seems to have been tempted more than once to cut and run—some of his creditors were scoundrels, he thought, deserving nothing. He cursed them in private. But Mark Twain was a man of public gestures, and he let it be known that he would travel around the whole world, old as he was and ill as he was, and that he would lecture and lecture until every creditor was paid in full. Privately, he did not think it could be done, but the newspapers cornered him, and he made a bold front of it: "The law," he told them, "recognizes no mortgage on a man's brain, but I am not a business man, and honor is a harder master than the law." So, and at Rogers's insistence and with Rogers's encouragement, he made the trip, and preserved the image of Mark Twain among his admirers.

While he was away, Rogers handled Clemens's business affairs, alternately fighting off and paying off creditors, investing for him in copper and railroads and oil, so that by 1900, when the Clemens family returned to the United States, their debts were done away with, and they were back where Clemens always wanted to be, on the road toward wealth. But by that time he was really ill and old and bitter. While they had been away in Europe his oldest daughter had died;

and he learned that his youngest daughter was an incurable epileptic; and he saw that Mrs. Clemens was worn and weak and ill, and that embittered him more. "I cannot think," he wrote, "why God, in a moment of idle and unintelligent folly, invented this bastard human race. And why after inventing it, he chose to make each individual in it a nest of disgusting and unnecessary diseases, a tub of rotten offal."

The tenor of Clemens's life now changed. He who had been a family man, fond of home and the discrete circle of friends at Hartford, became now (as he had been earlier during his Western years) a man of masculine affairs, in which Mrs. Clemens and his daughters had little share. Of his devotion to Mrs. Clemens there can be no doubt; but she was ill and his presence tired her, so that he was allowed to see her during one awful period only for a few minutes each day. But he spoke often of her in public—in after-dinner speeches and lectures which he was increasingly called on to give; his friends and his audiences admired him for the depth of his admiration for his wife. He was Mark Twain, a public man, and his husbandly devotion became a public thing. His whole life was public now—he enjoyed being seen with Rogers and William Rockefeller at prizefights; he was proud when Stanford White took him to Jim Corbett's dressing room at the New York Athletic Club; he liked being seen riding down Fifth Avenue in her new automobile with Henry Rogers' attractive daughter-in-law. He liked especially the trips on Rogers' steam yacht, the *Kanawha*, and the poker and horseplay and good masculine fun that was there enjoyed.

Samuel Clemens had always wanted to be a millionaire, and now he was, vicariously: he lived like one, and he was seen often in the company of bona fide, class A, genuine products. One part of him hated it; the other part lapped it up greedily: he became more and more and more spoiled—a kind of private jester to the Rogers and the Rockefellers and the Flaglers and their friends. He called Andrew Carnegie St. Andrew, and Carnegie called him St. Mark, and each knew that the joke of it was that neither was saintly at all. Their jokes together were fun. Because Carnegie was a Scotchman,

Mark Twain held him responsible for supplying him with Scotch whiskey; but in private Mark Twain wrote Carnegie down as a less than benevolent, at the same time that in public he let himself be publicly used.

It was good for these wealthy men to be seen with a person so popularly loved as Mark Twain. They liked him, and they were all boyish brigands together, each in his kind; but it was also good for their public image. He rode with them to public hearings at which their honesty was impugned; he was seen with them at testimonial banquets and at sporting events. Surely, no man could be all bad, if Mark Twain liked him. And Clemens did genuinely like these people, and like being seen with them. Newspapers might know Rogers as a "Standard Oil fiend," but Clemens knew him as a friend, and was proud to be privileged to drop in on him or on other members of his family whenever he wished, to be petted and waited on and spoiled. Rogers was the "only man I care for in the world; the only man I give a damn for." He was "lavishing his sweat and blood to save me and mine from starvation and shame."

But knowing the Rogerses and their friends was not something which Clemens shared with his family. The Clemens girls seem not to have known the Rogers girls at all, and Mrs. Clemens seems only to have met Mrs. Rogers when the Rogers yacht was put at Clemens's disposal so that he could take his ailing wife away from the New York heat for the summer. It may be that Clemens unconsciously believed that by keeping his family secluded, away from the kind of public and fawning life which he led, he was keeping them from contamination. For he became pulled quite asunder, more bitter than he had ever been, in scorn of all mankind—that damned human race—and in conscience-ridden condemnation of himself: "What a man sees in the human race," he said, "is merely himself in the deep and private honesty of his own heart. Byron despised the human race because he despised himself. I feel as Byron did and for the same reason."

His increasing bitterness distressed Mrs. Clemens, who not many weeks before she died in 1904 wrote him a note which is filled with wifely devotion and genuine concern, wishing that he would show the world the sweet, dear, tender side that she knew. But then she died, and he exploded, and later was to write: "there is *nothing*. There is no God and no universe; . . . there is only empty space, and in it a lost and homeless and wandering and companionless and indestructible thought. And God, and the Universe, and Time, and Life, and Death, and Joy and Sorrow and Pain only a grotesque and brutal *dream*, evolved from the frantic imagination of that insane thought." And what a thing was man: "Hypocrisy, envy, malice, cruelty, vengefulness, seduction, rape, robbery, swindling, arson, bigamy, adultery, and the oppression and humiliation of the poor and helpless in all ways have been and still are more or less common among both the civilized and uncivilized peoples of the earth."

This world, he wrote, "is a strange place, an extraordinary place, and interesting. . . . The people are all insane, the other animals are all insane. Man is a marvelous curiosity. When he is at his very best he is a sort of low grade nickle-plated angel; at his worst is unspeakable, unimaginable; and first and last and all the time he is a sarcasm. Yet man, blandly and in all sincerity, calls himself 'the noblest work of God.' . . . He believes that the Creator is proud of him; he even believes that the Creator loves him; has a passion for him; sits up nights to admire him; yes, and watch over him and keep him out of trouble."

Like Walt Whitman, he compared man to the animals: "indecency, vulgarity, obscenity—these are strictly confined to man; he invented them. Among the higher animals there is no trace of them. They hide nothing; they are not ashamed. Man, with his soiled mind, covers himself. . . . Man is the Animal that Blushes. He is the only one that does it—or has occasion to. . . . Of all the animals man is the only one that is doing it. Man is the only animal that deals in that atrocity of atrocities, War. He is the only one that gathers his brethren around him and goes forth in cold blood and with calm pulse to exterminate his kind. . . . Man is the only slave. And he is the only animal that enslaves. . . . Man is the only Patriot. . . . Man is the Religious Animal. . . .

He is the only animal that has the true religion—several of them. He is the only animal that loves his neighbor as himself and cuts his throat if his theology isn't straight."

> "Onward, Christian soldiers
>   Marching unto war,
> With the flag of progress
>   Going on before. . . .

> "On, ye true believers
>   Put them into flight
> Charity dispensing
>   Mixed with dynamite."

Clemens was bitter and discouraged, and he began detailing his bitterness for posterity, in writings which would not be read for a hundred years, for he dared not speak these thoughts in his own day, to his friends who, he thought, were as crass and sinful as he. The world was greatly with him, and it pulled him apart. The face he showed was a clown's face, a serious and sharp-tongued clown, but one not to be held responsible for what he said. The aging, compromising Mark Twain does not present a pretty picture, but perhaps no man does. His writing deteriorated during these late years. It became pointed and plain, saying what it had to say with vigor, but with no overtones, only anger and despair as he whipped himself and whipped his friends and contemporaries in frenzies of disgust.

In public, he posed and preened, spoiled and pampered. He played the wounded lion, and displayed his wounds for all to see. He was a funny man, good to have around to laugh or grouse with. He must have known that in an important sense he had sold out, and that respectworthy people (like Stephen Crane, for one) were beginning to scorn him as a public clown. Soon younger men like Sherwood Anderson, Waldo Frank, and Van Wyck Brooks would be speaking of the wastage of his powers—his half-baked, half-believed, half-buffoonery. Ten years after his death, Van Wyck Brooks gave reasoned explanation of what Clemens had allowed to be done to the genius of Mark Twain. His indictment has needed only small revision even in the almost fifty years since it was first made. Like many of his countrymen, before or since, Clemens did sell out—it was, and perhaps still is, the customary, if not the expected thing for a man to do.

But there were, of course, other things—including growing older—which contributed also to what seems to me the spiritual bankruptcy of Mark Twain—it had better be said, of Samuel Clemens—after he gave himself over to Rogers and his friends and his influence and his wealth and tempting ministrations, in exchange for or in gratitude for release from financial bankruptcy. Hardly anything that Clemens wrote after 1890 is moving or aesthetically right, not even "Eve's Diary" which is marred as he submits even his grief over the death of his wife to conventional poses and what he must have recognized as sentimental silliness. He continued to write occasionally well, for he was a professional who knew his business; and he became perhaps even a little more popular than he had been before, and that may be because he wrote what other people thought, or what other people thought he should write. He hardly ever attacked anyone except patsies, like Boss Tweed and Jay Gould and missionaries, whom it was fashionable to attack; his snub of Gorki was two-faced and just as public as it could be; his recriminations against King Leopold were as safe from public opposition as was his public friendship with Booker T. Washington and Helen Keller and little girls—and, oh, that poor cabman who dared overcharge a Clemens retainer!

Clemens of course was old and he had reasons in plenty for his sorrow and his bitterness; in a literary sense, his anger was the best thing left to him, when it was real and lyrically explosive, as the anger of a later, also aging, Ezra Pound was explosive and often lyric. What charm was left was a learned charm, carefully maintained, with an entrepreneur's canny skill. The wastage of his powers of which Brooks was to speak came, I would think, now—not in those early years, or as a result of traumata from those early years, of growing up in midland America or searching wealth in the Pacific west, and certainly not during those years in the seventies and the eighties when he did his best work, but in the almost twenty years which followed when he found himself controlled by, and loyally liking, a new set of counsellors—not Howells so much any more, not Twichell in Hartford who presided at marriages and funerals, and on whom Rogers and Clemens played boyish tricks, but men of wealth (malefactors was not a word which Clemens would use in describing them) who made it profitable for him to be their private jester and public companion.

And of course his writing suffered, for one does not write well under duress, even when one accepts and is partly pleased by the conditions of duress. Surely, it was the humanitarian rather than the critic in Leslie Fiedler which allowed him to name *Pudd'nhead Wilson* as Mark Twain's second best book. *The Mysterious Stranger* was put together from what Clemens never quite finished; *What Is Man?* turned out to be as jejune in its way as *Captain Stormfield's Visit* was in its; and the writings that were so bitter that they could not be made public for a hundred years, as now issued, turn out to be Mark Twain's last joke—just more of the same complaints of man's inadequacy, with only a snigger of sex added, and just a little excrement. The shimmer was gone, and the magic which transformed Huck and the great river into things which are not forgotten because never completely spoken, and which are set before us with more love than anger. It may be charitable to think that Mark Twain had been dead for over a decade—make it sixteen years!—when the twentieth century opened, and that it was a pasteboard mask through which Clemens spoke during the ten years more that Clemens lived in masquerade. But that will not do, because it was Clemens who spoke all the time—a forgotten man in our literature, this Samuel Clemens, who must have the praise for creating Mark Twain and the blame also for allowing him to be tempted toward corruption. Mr. Mark Twain, he told the truth, mainly; but not Mr. Clemens.

The Pisan Cantos
The Form of Survival

WALTER SUTTON

The poetic record of an almost shattering experience, the poems of *The Pisan Cantos* (1948) are the culmination of all that had gone before in Ezra Pound's life and work. Conceived in humiliation, when Pound's will to endure, to survive intellectually and aesthetically, was put to its greatest test, these eleven cantos (74–84) [1] stand as a victory won from defeat—a pledge of aspiration wrung from extremity.

When they are considered both as a distinct group and as a part of a major work, an epic, they also provide a focus for questions of form. The most directly personal of all Pound's poems, the Pisan cantos are the only ones that give the reader a satisfying sense of the man behind the work, as distinct from the *persona* or *personae* of the other poems. For this reason they raise questions about the modernist requirement of impersonality and objectivity, whether set forth in Eliot's impersonal theory of poetry and his idea of the objective correlative or in Pound's conception of the mask and the ideogram.

As a new and climactic addition, the Pisan cantos also provide a fresh perspective for viewing the formal organization of *The Cantos* as a whole. Although Pound's temperamental distaste for logical or chronological organization makes for difficulty in reading, much of what has been regarded as fragmentation and inconsistency in *The Cantos* is the result of necessary changes and adjustments in the poet's conception of his work during successive periods of his life. Though these shifts in outlook and interests have detracted from the unity and coherence of the poem, they have not resulted in formlessness, as has often been charged. *The*

Cantos is neither a perfectly integrated work with the kind of form desired by Yeats ("full, sphere-like, single") nor merely a collection of shards or fragments.

Certain unifying devices present from the beginning persist throughout the cantos. Among these the two most important, and closely related, are the quest theme and the author's distinctive view of history. The image of the Odyssean voyage, which Pound introduces in the first canto, supplies the main strand of thematic continuity for the work, which can best be understood as an epic (a "poem with history," in Pound's definition) focused on the artist's quest for values in the modern world. As a voyager in the stream of history (chiefly Western) from the classical past to the present, Pound presents an unchronological, highly personal view of a process in which there has been a deepening decay of standards from the classic age of Greece and Rome, with their high cultures; through the Middle Ages, which still preserved a semblance of cultural unity through the influence of the Catholic Church; through the Renaissance, which saw the rise of capitalism (the modern version of *usura*) and the breaking of feudal communal ties; into the modern period, with the disruptive forces of mass revolutions and world wars.

But collectively the cantos have a positive and optimistic as well as negative emphasis. Pound not only condemns the forces that have corroded communal bonds. He also points to historical periods (the Confucian age in China; the Revolutionary period in America) and exceptional persons (princes, public servants, ethical teachers, incorruptible artists) as models of the values he is eager to promote. Pound is in fact attempting to provide specifications and a manifesto for a new and better culture deriving from the best and most enlightened values of a heritage that he has sifted and graded in a highly eclectic and individual way.

The first substantial installment of the poem, A *Draft of XVI Cantos* (1925), reveals the pattern of Pound's initial conception of his projected work. Spanning the centuries between the Homeric age and the First World War, the group begins with the descent of Odysseus into the underworld and continues through successive cantos that praise such heros as Sordello, El Cid, and Sigismundo Malatesta, condemn the rise of usury and its attendant corruption, point to the wisdom of Confucius as a saving norm, and descend again, this time to the hell of the modern usurers, loathsomely represented by the munitions mongers and profiteers of the First War. The concluding canto (16) brings the poet out of hell, bathing in a lake of acid to free himself of the hell ticks, and then provides a sudden vision of an "oasis" as he passes into the quiet air of a "new sky" and sees, as ideals from the past, "the heroes, / Sigismundo, and Malatesta Novello, / and founders, gazing at the mounts of their cities." Although the ideal city gives way to the violence of the War and the Bolshevik revolution before the canto ends, it persists as a tenacious image of Pound's vision of a renewed culture.

By the time these first sixteen cantos were reprinted in A Draft of XXX Cantos (1930), the world was suffering an international depression widely regarded as the final convulsion of the capitalistic system. Eleven New Cantos: XXXI–XLI (1934) reflects the economic preoccupation Pound shared with his contemporaries in this period of crisis, as he turned back to the Period of the American revolution and early republic for guidelines for his time. In contrast to the embracing perspective of the first sixteen cantos, these eleven are given over largely to portraits, drawn from correspondence and biographies, of Thomas Jefferson and John Adams as disinterested public servants and leaders, dedicated to the task of achieving the common good and opposed to usurious private banking interests.

Although motifs from the earlier cantos persist, The Fifth Decad of Cantos (1937), like the group preceding, is dominated by Pound's economic interests, here focused on the Guild Socialism of A. R. Orage, editor of the New Statesman, and the social credit theory of Major C. H. Douglas. Pound absorbed elements of the radical theory of both these men into his own developing "Jeffersonian-Confucian" viewpoint. In the Fifth Decad Pound groups Douglas and Orage with Mussolini (who had earlier been linked with Jefferson and Adams) as "constructive" men who seek to defend the common wealth from the predations of usurers. Canto 45 stands out in gemlike clarity amidst the splintered history of most of the cantos in the group as it details, systematically, the human and cultural costs of *usura*, which Pound brands a sin against nature.

Cantos LII–LXXI (1940), the largest group to be issued as a separate unit, appeared in a collection of 167 pages, with a table of contents that shows it to consist of two differing but thematically related "decads." The first, the "Chinese" cantos (52–61), presents in a highly selective and compressed fashion more than four millennia of Chinese history in which dynasty follows dynasty with a staccato rapidity not unlike the interminable "begats" of the Old Testament chronicles. Confronted with a kaleidoscopic "overview" of a vast and unfamiliar subject, the reader is not likely to achieve any sense of the pattern of Chinese history, although he can recognize that Pound is singling out for praise rulers who exemplify the Confucian virtues and attempt to conserve and renew the common wealth of the nation. In the Adams cantos (62–71), Pound is more successful in his effort to create poetry out of the materials of history. Even with the fragmentation of detail that had by this time become characteristic of his work, Pound's portrait of John Adams impresses the reader with a coherent sense of the personality and viewpoint of the man Pound admired as the "clearest head in the Congress" and an unselfish public servant who hated the "swindling banks" that had "ruin'd our medium" (71).

The link with the Chinese cantos is made explicit in Pound's repeated use, in the Adams cantos, of the *ching-ming* term and ideograph (to call *things* by their right *names*) to endorse Adams' habit of clear perception and plain speaking. At the end of Canto 70, Adams' statement "I am for balance" is followed by one of Pound's favorite ideographs, the sign to stand firm in the middle. Thus the American leader of the early Republic is identified with the Confucian emperors admired by Pound, with the difference that the historical context and the character of the American are more familiar to the reader and more fully specified by the poet. There are other important differences, not acknowledged by Pound, between the traditional monarchist view of the Chinese ruler and the progressive republican outlook of the (conservative) American revolutionary.

In the groups of cantos that followed the first sixteen Pound turned to history, under the pressure of events, and wrote poems in which the original Odyssean quest, with its classical context, persisted only as a largely submerged theme while he attempted to find answers to the economic dilemma of his time. With *The Pisan Cantos* (1948), another shift occurred, as the prison poet was forced to take account of his personal predicament and adjust to it. A political prisoner, he was a victim of history. But he was also a man alone, under duress, faced with the problem of survival, not so much in physical as in moral and psychological terms. Although the mythic and historical preoccupations of the earlier cantos were not left behind, in *The Pisan Cantos* Pound found it necessary to confront, existentially, the problem of the values upon which his own life depended. In doing so he considered more fully and directly than in any of his earlier work his relations with his fellow men and with nature and his vocation as an artist.

Besides being the most personal of all Pound's poems, these cantos are the only ones in which there is a definite sense of place, of the poet's immediate environment as it impinges upon him inescapably. The place is the American Army's prison camp ("Disciplinary Training Center") near Pisa, where Pound was confined from May to November, 1945—for three weeks in a steel cage—before being flown to Washington, indicted for treason, and remanded to St. Elizabeth's hospital. Living in the midst of murderers, rapists, thieves—the Army's most hardened offenders—Pound looks out, in these cantos, upon the ruins of not only Mussolini's Fascist order in Italy, which he had supported, but the "broken ant-hill" of Europe. Nostalgically but unsentimentally he mourns the loss of better days and gone companions. Resisting the crushing pressures of prison life, he struggles to sustain himself through his contacts with nature, his memories of the past, and his commitment to art. Though his reforming and pedagogic spirit has not died, it is in abeyance. There is a continuation of the theme of *usura* as the source of social evil, but without the strident exhortations of the earlier cantos. What preaching there is introduces a new note of humility: "Pull down thy vanity . . ." (81).

There are, however, occasional eruptions of prejudice, including unfeeling allusions to the Nazi treatment of the Jews. There are also condescending and occasionally humorous references to "niggers" and "shades," as in "I like a certain number of shades in my landscape" (79). Intrusions of this kind disfigure the poetry and offend the reader. They are outweighed greatly, however, by passages in which Pound is at the height of his powers as a master of imagistic lyric verse.

Sometimes, in fact, the reader is impressed by the poetry and the sensibility it represents, even when he cannot share the poet's sympathies. *The Pisan Cantos* opens with the image of Mussolini and his mistress hung by the heels in Milan after having been killed by partisans. Regarding the Duce as a "twice crucified Christ," Pound identifies the lost leader with Malatesta as an architect of a visionary city.

> To build the city of Dioce whose terraces are the colour
>   of the stars.
> The suave eyes, quiet, not scornful,
>   rain also is of the process.
> What you depart from is not the way
> and olive tree blown white in the wind
> washed in the Kiang and Han
> what whiteness will you add to this whiteness,
>   what candor? (74)

The dream is that of Pound, not Mussolini (upon whom it is projected), and the compelling power of the lines derives from the intensity of the poet's aspiration, not the discredited leader's. The vision of a renewed order, based on the poet's Jeffersonian and Confucian ideals, seems defeated, but it is one that Pound will not let go:

I surrender neither the empire nor the temples
                                           plural
    nor the constitution nor yet the city of Dioce

The social idealism implicit in Pound's secular dream is admirable, even though he had mistakenly identified his ideal with the program of a shoddy Fascist regime.

The identification with Odysseus with which Pound had begun *The Cantos* is continued but appropriately with a greater emphasis on the misfortunes and adversities of the hero as "noman" and "a man on whom the sun has gone down" (74). Pound compares his ordeal in the cage made of steel air strip with Odysseus' wreck before being cast up on the shore where Nausicaa found him:

hast'ou swum in a sea of air strip
        through an aeon of nothingness,
    when the raft broke and the waters went over me (80)

But more significantly, Pound appears in these cantos in his own person, self-designated as "Old Ez" (itself something of a *persona*, as his old friend William Carlos Williams suggested). He describes his experiences and thoughts as a prisoner, looks back at his past life, and sums up his present views. He who had been "hard as youth sixty years" (80) is forced to recognize the toll of age and deprivation. He speaks of fatigue "deep as the grave" and notes, in an entirely new personal manner, "The loneliness of death came upon me (at 3 P.M., for an instant)" (82). The second last of these cantos ends with the impatient plea "Oh let an old man rest" (83). Yet there is a dignity and basic disinterestedness in Pound's acceptance of his situation:

        Ols Ez folded his blankets
    Neither Eos nor Hesperus has suffered wrong
        at my hand (79)

There is always the pressing reality of the prison into which he has been thrust, "with Barabbas and 2 thieves beside me" (74). Looking about him, he reflects, "So lay men in Circe's swine-sty" (74). But these men are his companions, and as a reject himself, a defiant outsider like Villon (whom he had long admired). Pound shares their hatred and contempt for the grand offenders who wield power in a corrupt society:

> and the guards op/ of the . . .
> > was lower than that of the prisoners
> "all them g.d. m.f. generals c.s. all of 'em fascists" (74)

Though his ties lie elsewhere, Pound recognizes that humanity and charity are "to be found among those who have not observed / regulations" (74). It was a Negro fellow prisoner who had made him a writing desk from a packing case. The Confucian virtue of "filial, fraternal affection" which Pound praises as the "root of humaneness / the root of the process" (74) is to be found among what society regards as its dergs as well as in higher places.

But this recognition is not enough to ease the desolation of an artist, no longer young, cut off from everything that had made up his life and cast into a degrading confinement. Thrown so drastically on his own resources, he sustains himself through his enforced contact with nature and through memories of old places and old companions. The night sky with its constellations seen through the smoke hole of his tent is a link with the primitive world of the classics. It is nature not through Homer (a la Pope), but nature encountered as closely and immediately as a cultured Homeric Greek (not an unlettered primitive) would see it. There is a new intensity of *contact* in Pound's observation of "the smell of mint under the tent flaps / especially after the rain," the white-chested Martins on the barbed wire of the fence, the neat house of clay built under the tent roof by "Brother Wasp." "When the mind swings by a grass-blade," Pound comments, "an ant's forefoot shall save you" (83). And he acknowledges the saving power of a bond with the birds he fed and the lizard, which, as he says, "upheld me" (74). There is also a sensitivity to the beauties of nature, especially in its freest and most accessible forms, the clouds, which Pound notes repeatedly, with the judgment that "The Pisan clouds are undoubtedly various / and splendid as any I have seen" (77). And finally, in the last of the cantos (84), the affirmation

> Under white clouds, cielo di Pisa
> out of all this beauty something must come

More importantly, since Pound is essentially a humanist, he finds solace in memories of old friends and companions, many now dead and cited as "lordly men . . . to earth o'ergiven" in a line revived from his early translation of the Anglo-Saxon poem "The Seafarer." Among these men, both the dead and the living, remembered as precursors or leaders of the modern revolution in the arts, are Yeats (mentioned sometimes as Uncle William), Henri Gaudier-Brzeska (friend and promising abstract sculptor, lost in the First World War), James Joyce ("Jim the comedian singing"), Ford Madox Ford (formerly Hueffer, familiarly called Fordie), William Carlos Williams (a close friend since their student days at the University of Pennsylvania), Wyndham Lewis (the artist-novelist and fellow Vorticist whose portrait of Pound hangs in the Tate Gallery), T. E. Hulme (fellow leader of the Imagist movement, like Gaudier-Brzeska, killed in the First War), E. E. Cummings (the "kumrad"), Henry James (not a friend, but glimpsed and remembered as a link with the past), and that old friend and former ally T. S. Eliot (often called the Possom, sometimes tse-tse).

Pound characteristically finds his greatest stay in his commitment to beauty and his sense of identity as an artist. He quotes and later repeats Aubrey Beardsley's observation that "beauty is difficult" (80). He remembers the Philistine neglect of the first edition of Fitzgerald's *The Rubaiyat of Omar Khayyam*, which "lay there till Rossetti found it remaindered at about two pence" (80). He regrets having neglected an opportunity to meet Swinburne ("my only miss"), not simply for Swinburne's sake but because Swinburne had seen Landor plain (82). He thinks of Whitman, ignored and rejected in his own time—"exotic, still suspect / four miles from Camden" (82)—and quotes two verses of the mocking bird's song of frustration and grief from "Out of the Cradle Endlessly Rocking": "O troubled reflection / O Throat, O throbbing heart." He thinks of himself, rejected and looking out at a ruined world, but still the artist: "As a lone ant from a broken ant-hill / from the wreckage of Europe, ego scriptor" (76). And he invokes the image of "the rose in the steel dust" (74) as a symbol of the beauty abstracted and ordered through art, just as the steel filings are ordered by the power of the magnet.

The commitment to poetry, and confidence in its power, is not a new attitude for Pound. He had earlier voiced the same sentiment in the face of the disillusion of the First World War, in the "Envoi" of *Hugh Selwyn Mauberley* (1920). But in *The Pisan Cantos* the belief in art is combined with a belief in the human capacity for endurance and love. What is most striking, perhaps, about these poems is a persistence of confidence in the midst of conditions that had brought Pound to the brink of disintegration during his ordeal in the cage. The affirmation here is based on the bedrock of human amity and love. It is what remains as an unquenchable inner resource when a cultured, humane man is stripped of his accustomed associations and his place in the world. "Nothing matters," Pound repeats, "but the quality of the affections" (76, 77). He develops the theme in the traditional lyric (reminiscent of the "Envoi" in *Mauberley*) which begins:

> What thou lovest well remains,
> >   the rest is dross
> What thou lov'st well shall not be reft from thee
> What thou lov'st well is thy true heritage   (81)

The following admonition of humility before the green world ("Pull down thy vanity") leads into a contrasting statement of humanistic pride in having tried as a man to realize his ideals in action:

> But to have done instead of not doing
> >   this is not vanity
> To have, with decency, knocked
> That a Blunt should open
> >   To have gathered from the air a live tradition
> or from a fine old eye the unconquered flame

This is not vanity.
       Here error is all in the not done,
all in the diffidence that faltered.   (81)

Although *The Cantos* from the beginning represented a humanistic quest for values in the modern world, the Pisan cantos differ from all that had preceded in their focus on an irreducible personal integrity as the necessary foundation of the poet's values and attitudes—subject to human error though these might be.

Quite apart from Pound's idiosyncratic technique of fragmented rather than sequential presentation (which has long been the subject of criticism), the shifts in his viewpoint and in his preoccupations during the three decades covered by the first eighty-four cantos inevitably detract from the unity of the poem as a whole. But these changes, which sometimes are very abrupt, as in the new direction assumed in the *Eleven New Cantos* (1934), are perhaps more appropriate for a modern epic than a classical unity of subject and tone would be. For *The Cantos* is obviously a poem written "in process" by a poet aware of the problems of historical novelty and change and of the difficulties of maintaining his sea legs as a voyager in the stream of twentieth-century culture. When one considers the misfortunes that befell him, one recognizes the achievement of this Odyssean wanderer in surviving at all.

The mode of expression in *The Pisan Cantos* also violates the modernist requirements of objectivity and dramatic detachment which Pound, like Eliot, had long supported. His dropping of the mask in these poems, his speaking forth in his own person of his deprivation and his rewards, has resulted in a poetry of greater emotional depth and intensity, perhaps of greater authenticity, than much of his earlier purer, more technically consistent work. Besides a current of deep feeling, new in his poetry, and a lyricism reminiscent of his early poems, there is a sense of the poet as a human presence behind the moving words. In his early essay "Vorticism" (1914), Pound had referred to his assumption of a sequence of masks, or *personae*, as a search for selfhood and "sincere self-expression" in the flux of modern life. It might be said that the long quest ends successfully in the incongruous setting of the concentration camp at Pisa as the prison poet defines and presents *himself* in his present world before his readers. For all their effect of fragmentation, these poems are informed by Pound's indomitable will to endure as a man and to persist in his work in the face of great odds.

Philip Larkin

HOW DISTANT

How distant, the departure of young men
Down valleys, or watching
The green shore past the salt-white cordage
Rising and falling

Cattlemen, or carpenters, or keen
Simply to get away
From married villages before morning.
Melodeons play

On tiny decks past fraying cliffs of water
Or late at night
Sweet under the differently swung stars,
When the chance sight

Of a girl doing her laundry in the steerage
Ramifies endlessly.
This is being young,
Assumption of the startled century

Like new store clothes,
The huge decisions printed out by feet
Inventing where they tread,
The random windows conjuring a street.

Vivian de Sola Pinto

INDOMITABLE CITY—LONDON 1943-1946

For William Van O'Connor

I

LONDON IN 1943

The sultry grey of London skies
on summer evenings . . . sudden cool green
of foliage in quiet Bloomsbury squares:
those Georgian houses with the grace
of fanlight, pillared portico:
That is the poetry; then the brave prose;
the little shops, the pubs, the posters
shouting for War Loan, crying for help for Russia,
old scrawls on the walls
screaming for a Second Front.

Gaps in the straight line of grimy houses:
direct hit there in nineteen forty one.
Peer down into the naked
cellar into the rubble.
Lovely the jagged broken walls
with old yellow and blue wallpaper flapping,
bright in the evening sun.

Peacefully shines the water
in the great tank nearby
(145000 gallons)
painted with scarlet and yellow stripes.

Ah, London,
once in those distant

poisonous nineteen thirties
you were a dreary deadly hag bedizened
with gilded cerements of history,
with shining, stinking sheaths of lust and greed.

Fire struck you from the skies,
clean fire of reality,
shattered your smug and smirking normality,
blasted away your hundred million lies.

This was a miracle . . .
dry bones have lived again.

The nightmare Death-in-life is dead and in her place
an invincible old woman,
an indomitable old queen.

II

POST-WAR ODE
1946

Walking at midday through the ruined city
I heard broken arches weep, shattered walls moaning,
    I heard the wailing
    of ghostly sirens,
the dull crash of a thousand phantom bombs;
    ironical tall weeds were growing
    out of the gashed foundations.

Then from the burning pavement rose a maiden
And in the sun her precious hair was streaming,
    I saw her dazzling
    white skin, her brilliant
eyes that were blue as ice, royal as flame,
    terrible her glance, from her scarlet
    lips flowed holy music:

"They sacrificed me when they built the city,
with my bright blood they sprinkled the foundations,
    crushing my body's flower
    with loads of gold and iron,

for centuries I heard the grinding wheels, the tramp
    of stupid feet, the buzzing
    of empty words above me.

Then in the night fell shafts of fire from heaven,
fountains of flame that smashed the iron buildings;
    the hard pavements were cloven,
    shattered the firm foundations,
and in my ancient tomb I heard and I rejoiced:
    out of the tomb I rose
    into the night of terror and darkness.

Now I am free: O son of man have pity,
bury me not again in the tomb of gold and iron:
    I bring you freshness and freedom,
    music, colour and ripeness."
So spoke the golden ghost to me at noon, the broken
    arches shouted for joy
    and dancing flowers sprang
    out of the gashed foundations.

Cockfight in Milo

KARL   SHAPIRO

I found it hard to eat, though since I had been living alone I had become fascinated by cooking. I undercooked and over-flavored everything, used curries by the pound, cayenne pepper, white pepper, coarse ground black pepper, salt crystals and the whole range of spices which came in symmetrical bottles from Myron's, the best grocery in Milo. Instead of eating, I made fancy drinks which I invented, vodka and sourkraut juice, which I named The Manifesto, vodka and borscht, The Wandering Jew, or studied out recipes for mulled wine, for which I bought special mugs (at the best hardware store in Milo). In desperation at my loss of appetite I drank raw eggs, to the horror of anyone who happened to be standing by. Sometimes I would beat up raw eggs with sherry, being careful to add plentiful splashes of cayenne. "I've got the rajas," I would tell people. "It's a mental disease of the stomach in which if you don't have enough hot pepper or curry you begin to yodel." However, I swilled quarts of milk and whipping cream in between the drinking and felt fine, all in all. Except for the sneaking suspicion that I was neglecting certain of my vital organs and overplaying others. Only I didn't know which ones, and didn't really give a damn.

I drank four raw eggs and a cup of cream and then made a martini into which I dropped a Mexican pepperino. Then I took the martini to the bathroom and shaved. I decided on a pair of dark corduroys instead of bluejeans, a deep red Vi-yella shirt and an old gray Harris Tweed jacket much too big, which I wore from time to time anyhow. At the last minute I decided to wear my pair of raw leather hunting boots which I'd picked up in Colorado one summer. I figured I was overdoing the costume, but then I didn't really know.

Grace almost didn't open the door when she saw me. Her Siamese cat skittered behind the refrigerator. I had not forgotten to rummage in my suitcase for a gift and I handed her a Florentine cigarette box which I presented encased in a sandwich bag. I knew she didn't smoke, so I said, "I know you don't smoke, but somewhere, somebody does." She took it out of the sack and she wanted to know what the picture was on the lid. It had something to do with Pompeii; there was a stylized volcano with a few streaks of reddish lava on the hillside, then a heavy line underlining the volcano, underneath which were two symmetrical horsemen facing each other. In between them were a few minute figures on foot, a man in a toga sheltering a woman and facing them some kind of messenger.

"This guy is bringing them the news," I said, "but it's obviously too late. The atom bomb has struck." Grace made her thanks without going into ecstasies.

"I have some bourbon. What would you like with it?" she asked. She was dressed in a dark dress. No bluejeans, but she had the foresight to avoid high heels, which she wore even to seminars. A weird one, I thought.

I had a stiff bourbon and water without ice. Grace took a weaker one. We talked about our summers, each avoiding the summer's truths, whatever they had been. The Siamese cat had recovered from his initial shock and patrolled the top of the sofa behind my back. I had lived with Siamese cats for years during my marriage and feared and hated their guts. My private opinion is that they are the lost tribe of Israel.

"Siamese cats are the lost tribe of Israel," I announced, and Grace smiled. But instead of letting her say she would remove the animal, I picked it up deftly behind me without looking, and placed it on my lap and stroked it between the ears. It didn't purr but it began to relax, and having won this terroristic victory the cat stepped down and went to appear on top of the television, which was still warm. It was growing dusky outside and I thought we might begin to try to find the Graindorge farm, where the cockfight was going to be.

"I know," said Grace at the door. "Let's take my car. It needs the exercise."

"Swell," I said, "but I have to get the bottle out of my glove compartment. In case of a freeze." Grace was now wearing a black cashmere sweater which I suspected was not the right attire, but I said no more about what to wear at a Milo cockfight.

I drove, exclaiming about her car. "A tight little bitch," I said, glancing at her with a metaphysical grin. Grace showed a row of improbably perfect teeth.

I had laid Spoof's map on Grace's pocketbook which was on her legs and I drove slowly west through the frayed edge of Milo which without warning became pure country. There was about fifteen miles of mere highway and autumn-rich red sorghum fields, yellowing corn fields, now and then a stand of Russian olive trees. Once I placed my hand on hers and wondered whether it wasn't her pocketbook. Her skin was as smooth and cool as patent leather and it was hard to tell them apart. She understood the map like an expert navigator and seemed to trust it implicitly.

I said suddenly, "You know that jerk Spoof. It would be just like him to draw a map that leads us directly into the largest hog-wallow in America—whatever a hog-wallow is." I was beginning to be suspicious.

"You really over-estimate Spoof," said Grace. "He wouldn't hurt a fly. He plays jokes to make a point about a friend but not to hurt him. It's his way of talking."

"Self-expression," I answered, becoming even more suspicious. "He's a director," I added, "and I hate directors. We'll see if that map pans out."

Grace gave me time to slow down before we came to the county road. The twilight had become blinding, indeterminate, and I blinked. To make matters worse, the dirt cut-off was orange with dust clouds. Grace suggested that this must be the road because of the amount of dust kicked up by cars. I decided to turn on all the car equipment. I rolled up my window (and she did hers), and asked her to switch on the air-conditioning, which I couldn't locate, and then I switched on the windshield wipers and pressed the squirter to wash the windshield. I could feel Grace relax, curiously, and imagined I felt a wave of warmth coming from her direction.

We jolted through the crepuscular countryside while Grace clocked the tenths-of-a-mile numbers on the speedometer. You could only see ditches by the roadside.

"Stop," she said suddenly, and then, "back up when you can see."

I backed up without seeing, into my own dust cloud, when I noticed a tiny hand-painted sign on a huge tubular mailbox which said Graindorge. I turned left into two deep dry ruts.

"Your transmission is getting scraped," I said grimly.

"Daddy will get me a new one," replied the graduate student, and turned away with a flutter. I floated the car up the ruts to the farm. It really wasn't dark enough to turn headlights either off or on and I thought we must be early. But all of a sudden the rut-road came to an end and we were driving on a lawn and could make out the silhouettes of farm buildings. It was dark except in the west sky which was a silky washy blue high up, dimming down to a purple and splayed out with violet and gold flecks and toning down to blackness.

"Which building do you think?" I asked.

She said nothing but pointed ahead to a bevelled shape of a barn, as certain as if she had grown up there. I moved the car over the lawn. It was as soft as if it were being carried. "You're not offended?" I asked.

She gave her all-American smile and answered, "Offended! At what!"

And just as the map said, there were all those cars lined up at crazy angles behind the barn: half-tracks, new and old Chevvies, Volkswagons, and at least three Cadillacs. There was also a collection of Hondas and Harley-Davidsons. I thought I spotted a few faculty cars. In one corner I saw a Citroën.

We were getting out when I said, pointing to the Citroen crouched in the grass, "That must be the Janiczek's crazy car." We went over to look at the windshield. Sure enough, it had the University sticker.

It was really pitch dark as we stumbled over the stubble to the back door. We hadn't time to knock. The door opened; a

man stood there and simply admitted us, with the words—
no smoking at all. It was a barn all right, squishy and crunchy
with hay, manure, mud, the sound of collared animals
grumping against wood stalls, and the overall atmosphere of
great urine poured from God knows how many great organs
of evacuation and procreation. Added to that was the yelling.

A corrugated iron lamp hung from a high rafter, making a
perfect circle of light over the pit and the circle of men and
women crowded around it. The rest of the barn was in
shadow. I edged up to the crowd and got a glimpse of black
feathers flashing high in the air and the glint of steel spurs. I
thought I smelled blood but couldn't be certain. The yelling
rose and fell around me. Grace clutched my elbow. I glanced
at her and thought her eyes had a glint in them as they
edged up closer. The man who had let us in the back door
came up to me and said, "You forgot to pay. Ten dollars." I
fished for my wallet and was surprised to find my hand
shaking. I figured I was being taken but it was no time to
argue. The farmer went back to his post at the door.

"Excuse me a minute," I said, "I want to ask that
guy . . ."

She appeared not to hear me but kept her eyes fixed on the
kicking, wing-slicing, beak-slashing birds. One had a hole in
its head as big as a nickle and blood was welling from the
wound; still he kept lashing out with his steel footgear. Their
handlers at opposite sides of the ring leaned into the circle
silently; everyone else was shouting for a kill, men and
women both clutching loose bills in their fists.

I didn't seek out the man at the door at all but began to
circle the pit, looking at backs and when I could, the fren-
zied faces. I passed behind Brom Janiczek and his wife, he
clutching an empty pipe in his teeth and she with an unlit
cigarette dangling from her lips. They didn't see me and I
passed on.

I had almost circled the crowd when I spotted Wanda
sitting on a bale of hay. She was wearing a black motorcycle
jacket with the usual stars and studs and was drinking something from a coke bottle. I got into a shadow and watched
her. She seemed to be alone but in a second Kaz materialized

beside her and without looking at her took the coke bottle from her hand and drank. Then he handed the bottle back to her, still with his eyes on the dying cock. I walked in front of the pair. "Advance to be recognized," I said to Wanda but really to Kaz. Kaz said nothing but nodded with a jerk of his head.

"You do get around, Ed," said Wanda. And added, "Bring somebody?" Her eyes roamed around the circle but she didn't see anyone she could pin on me.

"The cashmere sweater," I answered. "Next to the kid with the handlebar moustache." There was a centennial coming up in Milo and lots of males of all ages were taking advantage of the occasion to grow Wild West hair. In fact, it was being encouraged by the Chamber of Commerce. Next year the males would all go back to butch haircuts and business suits, except for the motorcycle fringe.

"She's pretty," said Wanda, swigging from the bottle. "Want some, Ed?" She handed me the bottle. I didn't relish drinking from the bottle that Kaz was also swilling but I took a slug to see what it was. Bourbon with a touch of coke. I took a good swallow.

"Good," I said. "See you Kaz." I thought for a moment before I said to Wanda, "Good cocking." I thought Kaz twitched or tensed but wasn't sure. "That's what the game is called," I added, pointing to the ring. The cock with the hole in its head was finally dead and there was a silence while money changed hands.

"Keep your fucking education to yourself," said Wanda and put her arm around Kaz. I wandered back to my date.

The Janiczeks had spotted Grace between matches and were flanking her when I got back. We all hugged sociologically and conspiratorially. Karen whispered into my ear, "We can see about three more kills before the cops come," and scrunched up her face and smiled.

"Do you mean it?" I asked. I didn't relish a ride to town in one of Milo's 1945 paddy wagons.

Brom added, "We're leaving at ten sharp," and looked at his wristwatch, which he wore on the inside of his wrist. I never can understand why anybody wears a watch that way.

It might be a gesture of self-protection. When you look at your watch your hand is in front of your face. "You and Grace come by our dig for a drink?" Brom called his house a Dig, as if it were some archaeological find.

"Let's do, Edsel," Grace said, not looking at me. She must have seen me while I was lurking around the bale of hay.

"Give us the signal when you go," I said. "How do you know?" I asked Brom abruptly.

Brom shushed me and whispered, "Gimpy Slezak, the Chief. He's on my payroll." He nudged me to save the details for later.

I took this to mean that the local police chief was contributing information to Janiczek's celebrated and long-unpublished study of the plains city. Brom had the confidence of all the city officials and access to all files as well as copious tip-offs and a warehouse full of inside dope. The clerks and political appointees trusted him as a loveable old university dope who eventually would put each and every member of the society on the map with flying colors. Brom subtly traded information from bureau to bureau, gossiping really, but no more than was necessary to keep his oar in. His knowledge of rape-murder cases, of which Milo had more than its just share, could have blighted whole suburban neighborhoods, had he wanted to use it. He didn't. I figured that Brom was really a collector, a librarian at heart, and that he would never draw the conclusions and lay the generalizations on the line which it was his profession to do. So Gimpy had tipped off the Janiczek's about this idiotic cockfight and the 10 P.M. raid.

I slipped my hand into Grace's; it was cool as marble and as soft as tissue paper. I felt the chill but didn't let go.

During the next bird battle there was a fight between a man and a woman at the side of the pit. Graindorge dragged the man by the collar to the door and opened it for the man to leave. He left. Nobody took much notice. There was the same yelling, waving of paper money, flashes of black feathers and red blood and white steel cock feet. I really didn't watch the fights but studied what glimpses of Kaz and Wanda I could get sitting on the hay across the circle. They

must have had an endless supply of bottles of coke; it seemed
to pass back and forth with the rhythm of a metronome. He
never touched her but she either leaned against him or lay
her hand in his lap. Once I thought I saw her stroking his
crotch but wouldn't swear to it. I felt a sudden queasiness
and suggested to Grace a breath of air. It was her turn to
look at her watch, a delicate platinum thing which seemed
painted on her matchstick wrist.

"Five minutes," she said, looking at me with big clear eyes.

"I'll get the bottle," I answered. I worked my way to her
car and worked my way back to the group. We sipped from
the bottle and coughed. Nobody interfered, including the
farmer-bouncer, who was now wandering back and forth.

"Time," said Karen in a low voice and nudged me. "Go
casually," she hissed. Another nudge.

We peeled off imperceptibly and Indian-filed through the
door.

"You go first," said Brom. "You know the house. Door's
always open."

Brom had to pump up his crazy Citroën which had some
sort of pneumatic springs which let the car down like a
balloon when he stopped. The red Buick floated around the
barn, into the ruts, and out onto the dusty county road. I
drove slowly to see if the Citroën would watch up. I saw the
smoke of headlights a quarter of a mile behind me and
decided it must be the Janiczeks, and I speeded up. And
about a mile from the highway, sure enough there passed one
state highway patrol car, then another, then the Black Maria.

"They really mean it, by God," I said. "Why don't they
let the bastards kill their chickens."

"Gambling is supposed to be immoral," said Grace vap-
idly.

I gave an empty laugh. "How is your friend?" she added.

"She's not my friend. She's not even my whore, Grace.
She's . . . she . . ."

"That you think you have to degrade yourself . . ." she
started, and looked out of the window silently all the way to
the dim-lit Janiczek's Victorian bungalow.

When I had turned the Buick's motor off, I said to myself,

"Degradation." I shifted in my seat and looked at Grace. "Since when do you preach?" I asked rhetorically.

"Please forget it, Ed," she answered, and added, "Isn't it a beautiful house?" It *was* beautiful, even in the dark. Huge old elm trees, already marked for slaughter because of the elm tree disease, guarded the lawn and shut out the moonlight. The house was brown and brown, dark brown trim on the lofty gently curvy windows and cornice and light brown the rest of the way. Brom and Karen had done the painting, and I felt a twinge of envy at their complicity, their coupledness. Tears came to my eyes but I kept them to myself.

"What did you make of the cocking?" I asked.

She fluttered again, looked toward the house and then back at me in the speckled shadow.

"I liked it," she said. "No, I loved it. I think it was honest. I don't mean gambling." She faltered. I waited. "It was animal," she went on. "Or maybe I just admired it. Anyway, I'm glad I went. And I'm glad you went. And I'm glad you asked me."

She shuddered slightly and my hand sought hers, both of which lay primly on the surface of her pocketbook. Her hands remained palm down on her pocketbook but she edged her body a fraction into mine. Without thinking, I ran my hand under her dress and up her thigh. If she had been marble she couldn't have felt it less. No muscle twitched, no limb stirred, the temperature remained the same.

I thought, Okay, Ice Maiden.

"They'll be here in a minute," she said, still as a statue, looking again at the lovely Victorian bungalow. Car lights announced themselves in the rear-view mirror and jounced neatly up the street a couple of blocks away. They grew bright to the point of blindness. I gripped Grace solidly so she wouldn't open the door. The headlights turned majestically into the Janiczek's driveway and coasted to a stop. But in the rearview mirror appeared new headlights. The Janiczek's headlights were turned off when the new ones approached slowly and began to turn into the driveway. I leaned over to the dashboard and switched on the Buick lights.

"Wanda and Kaz," said Grace, stiffening.

"How do you feel about some transactional psychology?" I said.

"In a minute, Ed. I want to fix my mask." She was redecorating herself in the dark. It didn't work and she switched on the top light. I watched the reconstruction in a daze. Grace was a master of the cosmetics department. I didn't feel that I had the sanction to criticize her but nevertheless thought, she's a live manikin, a store dummy, she's a clothes horse, she's a big-enough-to-fuck-doll. And I thought, while she was biting on a piece of Kleenex to get the excess off, no, she's a human being person. She's intelligent, she's pretty, but she grew up in a Frigidaire. She's on an ice floe and will never get off. And me, I was born in the Sahara with a craw full of sand and all I want is a drink.

We got out of our separate doors and went up the walk and entered the hallway of the Janiczeks.

"Kiss the totem pole, darling," I instructed. There was a truncated totem pole in the entrance way. Grace kissed it obediently, leaving a little trace of lipstick on an eagle's wing.

"I'm patriotic too," I said, and ran my hand down the phallic symbol which topped the fragment. We entered the living room which was empty but which had a small table in one corner. On the table was a crowd of gallon-sized whiskey bottles, glasses, ice bucket, and an unopened bag of pretzels. We both took bourbon and ice and sat down. I found myself breathing hard. From another room flamenco music started up and a stomping of feet.

"Let's have our drink," said Grace. I smiled at her and sipped.

"Apologies aren't that bad," Grace said out of the blue. "You know, Ed, you don't make a very convincing savage. People don't really take your savagery very seriously. You're like a gentle civilized person who has discovered—well, Villon or Walt Whitman. But it really doesn't go with you."

I bristled, thinking I was hearing echoes from her religious Ph.D. padrone and master.

"I'm not a *sauvage*," I answered, listening to the stomping of feet. "I'm a barbarian. It's quite a different style. I don't want to see the idols fall from behind my tree. I want to topple them with my own hands. I want to push." I waited.

Grace sat silent and I went on with my idea.

"I want the idols to fall but not to be buried. I want them like Rome in the Renaissance, the Forum all silted up but visible and grown over with vines. Me, I'm strictly baroque. I'm the baroquest son-of-a-bitch in history—in Milo, anyway."

I snuffed pleasurably into my drink.

"Well," I said, "of course, fallen beauty. Faisandage. Stink. Malaria in the Colosseum. Henry James. Oscar Darling. Astrology. You take Wanda. She digs astrology. Now, I ask you, what is better, the busted Victory of Samothrace or the whole one which I hoped to God nobody will ever see? Who wants to see the Acropolis in all its vulgar glory? Not me. I'll take it after the Turks took it. Just like it is right this minute, crawled over by the little old ladies from Dubuque and the toothless tourists of London and Sydney. A bomb crater, but with the bones bleached and blazing in the sun in rotten little fascistic Greece, Anno Domini 1984. Your idealism is for the birds. It's pure Germanic monomania which you are being converted to by your saintly Atwood Tremaine. For the love of God, as Poe would say, how can you take anybody seriously who is named Atwood Tremaine. He belongs to the paleontology of English Departments. He wipes his ass with parchment. He screws his wife with gauntlets on."

"And you?" asked Grace. She was not given to duelling and I was tagged off base and gave her a grateful smile.

"Let's go see the party," I said wryly.

We wandered through three rooms of books and maps, statues, ceramics, spiny spears once tipped with poison, huge dark red urns, modern paintings from the Milo Art Department, batiks and laces on wall-spaces, and stunted Japanese trees in tubs, all dead but striking in their littleness. We found the Janiczeks and Wanda and Kaz in the bedroom of the son who was away at Antioch for his junior year.

Brom had yanked back a huge glowing Navajo rug and the floor of the bedroom was bare. Kaz stood in the middle of

the room with arms folded, looking for all the world like a
flamenco dancer. His black motorcycle boots added to the
impression. Wanda lay on the bed as if she had been flung
there. The Janiczeks were standing and clapping in rhythm
and emiting *Oles!* at more or less appropriate times. Apparently Kaz was serious in his try to imitate the footwork. I,
doing a slow burn, wondered where he had picked up his
interest in this kind of thing. The guitar record buzzed like a
giant hornet; in the background of the record could be heard
the spontaneous plaudits of some audience who had once
witnessed whatever the performance was. Grace went to sit
on the bed next to Wanda. For some reason I admired the
gesture. When the guitarist approached an unidentifiable
speed toward the end of the recording, Kaz gave a motion of
helplessness and stood still and listened.

"You've got what it takes, Kaz," said Karen. A lump of her
hair, heavy and graying, had fallen to her shoulder from the
clapping. "You'd be a natural in Andalusia." Kaz lit a cigarette and said nothing. He always said nothing.

I noticed that Grace was sharing her drink with Wanda. If
Wanda was drunk she didn't show it. Her eyes were clear
with the dull sparkle of iron fillings.

"I listen to those records," said Kaz, "and I've seen Greco
on the tube. It's a real kind of dancing for a man. Nothing
fairy about that kind of dance. Great stuff." And abruptly he
walked out of the room.

The company reconvened in the living room, Kaz handing
a new drink to Wanda and Karen one to Brom. Brom felt he
had to give a small lecture about flamenco and told about
the *cante jondo*, deep song, he explained, and the erotic
gypsy style and the resemblance to the wailing chanting of
the Spanish Jews.

"It's tragedy," said Brom, "the tragedy of the bitten-off
peninsula, as Auden says."

"Therefore homosexual," I said, surprised that I had said
it.

The sociologists were always ready and willing to entertain
a far-out conclusion and looked at me expectantly. Everybody waited.

"I was in New Orleans before I went away," I started

badly, "and some guy who was a friend of the English Department or something, who owned a night club on Bourbon Street—anyhow he and his wife were flamenco buffs and they opened a real flamenco club with six honest-to-God Spaniards from Spain. It wasn't taking on too well but he was going to keep it open, no matter what. I went there one night at the end of the show and when the customers had left and the door was locked he had them run through the entire repertoire just for us, about six people." I stopped. I took a swallow. "I'd never seen it before really and didn't know what it was but I was damn impressed. I always thought Spaniards were dead people walking around and they convinced me. Beautiful and dead. Automatons. Fascists I guess, to the manner born. It's like what Lorca said about the Civil Guard. Always dressed in black, silent as the tomb, armed to the teeth, with high heels, the better to stomp the enemy. The cool killers whose greatest art is being gored in the groin by a bull trained to do exactly that."

I felt I wasn't quite on the right track and might be building up to a head-on accident, but I lurched on.

"Naturally, the Roman Catholics have always called Spain Our Second Sister in Christ. If Christ came down the stratosphere he's head straight for Madrid. The first thing he'd do would be to buy the most expensive box for the bullfights. He'd personally give extreme unction to Manolete. Maybe he'd heal his wound with his tongue. Why is it that black is the favorite color of the most bloodthirsty people? They kill so they can mourn. Then they kill some more. Then they dance it. Like the red and the black."

"What about the flamenco place?" Wanda asked in a dark voice.

I felt a sudden wave of drunkenness and felt as if I were in front of one of my classes. I knew I was going to be pedantic and knew I couldn't stop myself.

"As Lawrence said, noli me tangere. The dancing was the dancing of untouchables. Above the waist the little black straight jackets or the bare arms and ruffs of red for the females. All the action is from the waist down except for the snake-arms and the castenets. It was just like that Rilke poem where the Spanish dancer bursts into flame like a struck match. Only they strike the match with their feet because their life and their sex have all been forced into their feet, or rather their heels. It's the art, if I may disagree with Rilke, of stomping out the fire which they can only imagine."

"What were the women like?" Wanda asked.

"I recall two. One was short and stocky and quick as a spider. The other was tall, with an El Greco neck and a beautiful expressionless face. She was the star. She was titless but well-haunched and danced like a machine gun. The best-resurrected corpse I ever laid eyes on. She damn near drove holes in the stage with her heels but not a hair of her head even quivered. It was fantastic. The only live thing about them was the sweat under their arms. You could smell it. Incidentally," I added, "one of the best male dancers wasn't a Spaniard at all, but a Jew from Brooklyn. His name was Joel Spritz, or something."

I took a solid gulp.

"No, not homosexual. I take it back. The dances are asexual, one of the higher forms of jerking off. An attempt to resurrect Jesus, which in Spain is obviously hopeless." I wished that I could stop using the word "obviously" because I always used it when it obviously didn't apply. I used words like that for "charm," charm being a trick for disarming the enemy or decoying an authority.

"But after all, Brom," I said, "it's that kind of desperate ritual which leads to the explosion of art. You come to a dead end when you are being pursued by Jesus H. Christ or Francisco Franco and you damn well break out into Art or die. I think the Spaniards die because they like it that way. When they get a real poet like Lorca they shoot him in the balls. Even if he's queer."

I had run out of gas and Karen picked me up.

"I know what you mean, Ed," she said with a half-serious laugh. "I think I know. I feel sometimes we only admire the dead, and the deathly."

"It's true," Brom added. He always added to his wife's thesis, or put in some documentation to show their solidarity.

"If we could know the mystery of a dying culture we

might be able to save something of our own. All us high-brows are toxicologists and taxidermists."

"Love on the deathbed," I said and shot a look at Wanda.

"Get me another drink, Kaz," she said.

As Kaz crossed over me, he said, "I think you got a point there," and disappeared into the kitchen. I wondered which point had been picked up, or whether the remark was some kind of response to my unconcerted attack on the Kaz-Wanda team.

We dropped the flamenco seminar and went back to the cockfight. Grace wanted to know whether the police had actually raided the Graindorge farm and Brom told the whole story, who was taken in and who wasn't, how much money changed hands, how much Gimpy Slezak pocketed, the reason for the state of the roads around his house, which college students were not arrested and why.

"But the whole motorcycle set are in the cooler," Brom finished. "They are very essential to policing. They are care-fully arrested and attended, handled with kid gloves even when they have their teeth knocked out. Nothing is more necessary and—esthetic?—to the police than a fixed sub-culture or amateur criminals. The cops couldn't possibly func-tion without them. Of course, they are created by the cops, you know, Ed, the way a poem is. If the provincial public doesn't have a living example of the Wrong, the police die. They get tired of hanging around the public lavatory of the Pawnee Hotel waiting for some visiting salesman or some Milo professor to expose his penis erectus to the next pisser. They need a Group Enemy, just like the State Department." He laughed enjoyably.

"And what's so goddam funny about arresting people because they ride motorcycles?" Wanda wanted to know. She leaned forward pugnaciously. I started to answer when Karen took the ball.

"It's not motorcycles. Motorcycles used to be for cops and cops only. Cops—and couriers—in the First World War."

I sat back for a lecture which I was hoping against.

"Then the motorcycle racers took over, those guys who used to race in a wooden pit, like a cockfight. It was a big

wooden saucer and when the racers got to top speed they
rose horizontally around the walls of the pit. One spill killed
or maimed the whole lot of them. It was great sport. Then
there were the cross-country cycle racers, leaping ditches and
ploughing down corn and rupturing their spleens and other
equipment. Then they took to the highways. But that was
after the daredevil image was firmly implanted in the *public*
mind by the films." She underlined public. "It was when the
Public," and she capitalized *public*, "began to see the *evil* in
motorcycles," she giggled, "that the cyclists became Fallen
Angels."

"And just what the polizei ordered," added Brom.

Sociology forever, I thought.

Kaz had given the drink to Wanda, en passant, as it were,
and was again standing in the middle of the floor. He started
to drum with his heels and made a neat circle, standing in
place. There was no music and when he stopped he was
facing me. I looked him in the eye and slowly stood up and
gave him a push, saying to Grace, "Let's go."

I thought I might get a karate rabbit punch as I brushed
by him but nothing happened. I wondered if the rhythm of
my walk was slow enough as Grace and I went to the
vestibule, followed by the Janiczeks. I waved goodbye to
Wanda and smiled at Kaz. Grace used polite farewells to
everybody. We went out to the tight little Buick.

Leonard Unger

ON THE HEIGHTS OF GRIEF

On the heights of grief
The air is so rarefied
No word, no thought
Can be used carelessly.

At such altitude, in such atmosphere
Visibility is remarkable,
Clear beyond all wish,
Beyond all need.

Cloud, tree-top, boulder, water, cloud.

It is not possible to stay
Entirely in that dream,
Not possible to pass
Entirely to another.

One eye or the other
Is asleep or awake
And one ear hears still
The one heart beating.

Cloud, tree-top, boulder, water, cloud.

THAT OLD NEW YEAR

If, for want of a better word,
I were altogether "rational,"
I'd put a sign up in the
Back of my mind reading
NONSENSE—with reference (in smaller print)
To this being the last day of the year.

But it is really too bad
That it's such a low dark day
Without a crack in the heavy gray sky
Or a single twinkle of blue and gold
But only darkness growing darker
Into the New Year.

I can remember the very first time
One year ended and another year began.
I had never thought that the numbered name of the year,
Any more than my own face and my own name,
Would ever change. But it changed
And I was startled.

Since then, of course, my face
Has changed several times
And my name—well, my name—
This is to put the matter very mildly—
My name has changed beyond all recognition
And changes startlingly.

WHO'LL BE LIKE YOU?

When I read other people's poems
I am full of despair and admiration,
and gratitude, too, I should add.

It seems almost—mind you, almost
as if I wouldn't have to try to
write my own poems. After all,

everyone else was a child once, too,
and lives (or lived) in his or her
own body exposed to all weathers of

death and love. But when I think
of that favorite saying, "If I'll
be like him, who'll be like me?" —

then I know that I have to keep on
trying to be like myself—that is,
I want to. Even when I say hello

on the telephone, just hello, it's
nice if somebody recognizes my voice.
Just that much. If I recognize

your voice, then you have something
to say to me and you say it
better than anybody else could ever do.

Robert Penn Warren

BAD YEAR, BAD WAR: NEW YEAR'S CARD

"Without the shedding of blood there is no remission of sins."
—Epistle to the Hebrews, 9:22

That was the end of the bad war. The others—
Wars, that is—had been virtuous. If blood

Was shed, it was, in a way, sacramental, redeeming
Even those evil people from whose veins it flowed,

Into the benign logic of History, and some,
By common report, even the most brutalized, died with a shy

And grateful smile on the face, as though they,
At the last, understood. Our own wounds were, of course,
 precious.

There is always imprecision in human affairs, and war
Is no exception, therefore the innocent—

Though innocence is, it should be remembered, a complex
 concept—
Must sometimes suffer. There is the blunt

Justice of the falling beam, the paw-flick of
The unselective flame. But happily,

If one's conscience attests to ultimate innocence,
Then the brief suffering of those incidentally innocent

Can be regarded, with pity to be sure, as merely
The historical cost of the process by which

The larger innocence fulfills itself in
The realm of contingency. For conscience

Is, of innocence, the final criterion, and the fact that now we
Are troubled, and candidly admit it, simply proves

That in the past we, being then untroubled,
Were innocent. Dear God, we pray

To be restored to that purity of heart
That sanctifies the shedding of blood.

James Wright

A CENTENARY ODE
INSCRIBED TO LITTLE CROW, LEADER
OF THE SIOUX REBELLION IN MINNESOTA

I had nothing to do with it. I was not here.
I was not born.
In 1862, when your hotheads
Raised hell from here to South Dakota,
My own fathers scattered into West Virginia
And southern Ohio.
My family fought the Confederacy
And fought the Union.
None of them got killed.
But for all that, it was not my fathers
Who murdered you.

I don't know
Where the fathers of Minneapolis finalized
Your flayed carcase.
Little Crow, true father
Of my dark America,
When I close my eyes I lose you among
Old lonelinesses.
My family were a lot of singing drunks and good carpenters.
We had brothers who loved one another no matter what they
     did.
And they did plenty.
I think they would have run like hell from your Sioux.
And when you caught them you all would have run like hell
From the Confederacy and from the Union
Into the hills and hunted for a few things,
Some bull-cat under the stones, a gar maybe,
If you were hungry, and if you were happy,
Sunfish and corn.

If only I knew where to mourn you,
I would surely mourn.

But I don't know.

I did not come here only to grieve
For my people's defeat.
The troops of the Union, who won,
Still outnumber us.
Old Paddy Beck, my great-uncle, is dead
At the old soldiers' home near Tiffen, Ohio.
He got away with every last stitch
Of his uniform, save only
The dress trousers.

Oh all around us,
The hobo jungles of America grow wild again.
The pick-handles bloom like your skinned spine.
I don't even know where
My own grave is.

NORTHERN PIKE

All right. Try this,
Then. Every body
I know and care for,
And every body
Else is going
To die in a loneliness
I can't imagine and a pain
I don't know. We had
To go on living. We
Untangled the net, we slit
The body of this fish
Open from the hinge of the tail
To a place beneath the chin
I wish I could sing of.
I would just as soon we let
The living go on living.
An old poet whom we believe in
Said the same thing, and so

We paused among the dark cat-tails and prayed
For the muskrats,
For the ripples below their tails,
For the little movements that we knew the crawdads were
    making under water,
For the right-hand wrist of my cousin who is a policeman.
We prayed for the game warden's blindness.
We prayed for the road home.
We ate the fish.
There must be something very beautiful in my body,
I am so happy.

A WAY TO MAKE A LIVING

(from an epigram by Plato)

When I was a boy, a relative
Asked for me a job
At the Weeks Cemetery.
Think of all I could
Have raised that summer,
That money, and me
Living at home,
Fattening and getting,
Ready to live my life
Out on my knees, humming,
Kneading up docks
And sumac from
Those flawless clerks-at-court, those beautiful
Grocers and judges, the polished
Dead of whom we make
So much.

I could have stayed there with them.
Cheap, too.
Imagine, never
To have turned
Wholly away from the classic
Cold, the hill, so laid
Out, measure by seemly measure clipped
And mown by old man Albright

The sexton. That would have been a hell of
A way to make a living.

Thank you, no.
I am going to take my last nourishment
Of measure from a dark blue
Ripple on swell on ripple that makes
Its own garlands.
My dead are the secret wine jars
Of Tyrian commercial travelers.
Their happiness is a lost beginning, their graves
Drift in and out of the Mediterranean.

One of these days
The immortals, clinging to a beam of sunlight
Under water, delighted by delicate crustaceans,
Will dance up thirty foot walls of radiance,
And waken,
The sea shining on their shoulders, the fresh
Wine in their arms. Their ships have drifted away.
They are stars and snowflakes floating down
Into your hands, my love.

A SUMMER MEMORY IN THE CROWDED CITY

She came crying down to me
Out of the dim heaven
That I had been praying
Against all afternoon.
And I cannot say
That I loved the earth much
With its hay dust
That swaled my eyes closed.
And her voice did not have
The clear sweetness
We listen to
In the books of our childhood.
Shrill, nagging, beyond pity
Or anything like it,
She lashed down, just dying
To peck my eyes out.

Oh the darling,
She would have loved to get
Her hook in me.
She coiled back into a secret
Corner of the sky
And glared down,
A mere barn swift.

Well, you can't stand there.
I threw my forearms around
My face and bent forward,
Hunched into the barn
With Dave Woods
And his boy Slim Carter.
Did you see that bird, Dave?
Yes. Never mind. Look here,
Look at these pups.
They don't eat nothing but milk foam.
And look how fat they keep.

Somewhere a black woman
In absolute despair
Is cursing me blind
Gnashing jaw bone on shrunk
Gums. Dave, Slim, and I
Tossed her nightmare away.
We plodded into the barn.
We clattered the dung forks
Beneath the dank joists
Where surely, somewhere,
The nest curled over the blue
Veins of somebody's
Throat and wings.

We didn't look at each other.
What the hell are we supposed to do with those birds?
They clutter the whole barn,
They spend their days flailing the pinnacles of heaven
Where the angles do nothing
But pray and sing. Faugh!
We stabbed our forks
Into the cold cow pies
And shoveled them out.

Notes

The Continuing Need for Criticism   KRIEGER

1. An earlier version of this essay appeared as the opening article of the first issue of *Concerning Poetry*, I (Spring 1968), 7–21.

2. See Hassan's "The Dismemberment of Orpheus: Notes on Form and Antiform in Contemporary Literature," in *Learners and Discerners*, ed. Robert Scholes (Charlottesville, Va., 1964), pp. 135–65; "Beyond a Theory of Literature: Intimations of Apocalypse?" *Comparative Literature Series*, I (1964), 261–71; and *The Literature of Silence: Henry Miller and Samuel Beckett* (New York, 1967).

3. I expand this idea in my essay, "The Ekphrastic Principle and the Still Movement of Poetry; or *Laokoön* Revisited," *The Play and Place of Criticism* (Baltimore, 1967), pp. 105–28.

4. See Sutton's "The Contextualist Dilemma—or Fallacy?" *Journal of Aesthetics and Art Criticism*, XVII (December 1958), 219–29, and "Contextualist Theory and Criticism as a Social Act," ibid., XIX (Spring 1961), 317–25.

5. Douglas L. Peterson, *The English Lyric from Wyatt to Donne: A History of the Plain and Eloquent Styles* (Princeton, 1967), pp. 105–6.

6. Spellings have been modernized.

The Double Truth of Modern Poetic Criticism   MINER

1. At least everybody knows who has read William Van O'Connor's *Sense and Sensibility in Modern Poetry* (Chicago, 1948) or Frank Kermode's *Romantic Image* (London, 1961). Kermode's book has perhaps attracted the more attention, but O'Connor ranges far more widely, and without Kermode's polemic, or my own.

2. Kermode, pp. 150, 148.

3. From the earlier poems, for example, "You don't believe"; *The Everlasting Gospel*; from the later, *Milton* and most of the visionary writing.

4. "Dryden," *My Study Windows* (London, n.d.), Scott

Library ed., p. 265. This essay gives the best nineteenth-century criticism of Dryden after Sir Walter Scott.

5. "The Study of Poetry," *Essays in Criticism*, 2nd ser. (London, 1888), pp. 37, 41–42.

6. *Cross Currents in English Literature of the XVIIth Century* (London, 1965), p. 322.

7. "The Metaphysical Poets" [1921], *Selected Prose*, ed. John Hayward, Peregrine Books ed. (Harmondsworth, Mddx., 1963), p. 113.

8. *Morte d'Arthur*, ll. 251–53.

9. Wordsworth, *Intimations of Immortality*, ll. 145–46.

10. The Arnold quotations are taken from "To Marguerite—Continued," ll. 1–4, 15–16; and from *The Scholar-Gypsy*, ll. 203–4, 152, italics Arnold's.

11. William Butler Yeats, *The Trembling of the Veil* (London, 1922), p. 75.

12. Ibid., p. 80.

13. The symbol was of course an ideal French in origin; the literary ideal of myth was most influentially stated by Eliot's review of Joyce's *Ulysses*, "Ulysses, Order, and Myth," *The Dial*, LXXV (Nov., 1923), 480–83.

14. See my book, *The Japanese Tradition in British and American Literature* (Princeton, 1966), p. 66 and chap. 3, *passim*.

15. *Egoist*, 1 June 1914; *The Japanese Tradition*, p. 111 and chap. 5, *passim*.

16. Preface to Ezra Pound's *Certain Noble Plays of Japan* (1916); *The Japanese Tradition*, p. 253.

17. In Japan as well as in the West, the terms haiku, hokku, and haikai are often used interchangeably nowadays, although historically their implications (for discrete poems in 5,7,5 syllables, for the initial poem of a sequence, and for the sequence) are distinct.

18. *Fortnightly*, 1 September 1914; *The Japanese Tradition*, p. 114.

19. *Fortnightly*, 1 September 1914; *The Japanese Tradition*, p. 140.

20. Preface to *Certain Noble Plays of Japan*; *The Japanese Tradition*, pp. 256, 254, 253.

21. Konishi Jinichi, "New Approaches to the Study of the Nō Drama," *Tokyo Kyōiku Daigaku Bungakubu Kiyō* (1960), 1–34.

22. A further irony may be added. The late Fukase Motohiro, author of numerous studies of modern British and American literature, greatly esteemed these verses of Yeats and made a Japanese translation of them that was without irony.

An African Tragedy of Hubris: Thomas Mofolo's *Chaka*
GÉRARD

1. The language of Lesotho is more accurately described as southern Sotho. On the creative literature, see: G. H. Franz, "The Literature of Lesotho," *Bantu Studies*, IV (1930), 145–80; "Die vernaamste Basotho skryvers en iets oor hulle werk," *Die Basuin*, I (1930), 4, 12–15; "Die Literatur des Lesotho (Basutoland)," *Die Brucke* (Johannesburg), Wissenschaftliche Beilage, I (1931), 1–4, and ibid., II–IV (1932), 1–4; P. J. Coertze, "Die literatuur van die Basoeto," *Die Basuin*, III (1963), 6, 10–12; G. L. Letele, "Some Recent Literary Publications in Languages of the Sotho Group," *African Studies* III (1944), 161–71; M. D. Mohapeloa, *Letlole la lithoko tsa sesotho* (Johannesburg: Afrikaanse Pers-Boekhandel, 1950); M. Damane, *Marath'a lilepe* (Morija, Lesotho: Sesotho Book Depot, 1960); Albert Gérard, "Literature of Lesotho," *Africa Report*, XI (1966), 7, 68–70.

2. Not an uncommon occurrence in Black Africa. According to his brief autobiographical note printed by G. H. Franz, Mofolo thought he was born in August 1877. The correct date as found in the parish register at Teyateyaneng, the author's birthplace, was given me by the Rev. Albert Brutsch of the Missions Evangéliques de Paris. Biographical notices on Mofolo are numerous: anonymous obituary in *Bantu World*, 9 October 1948, 1; Georges Dieterlen in *South African Outlook*, LXXVIII (1948), 168–69, reprinted in *African Affairs*, XLVIII (1949), No. 190, 74–75; E. W. Smith in *Africa*, XIX (1949), 67–68; Peter Sulzer's introduction to his German translation, *Chaka der Zulu* (Zurich, 1953); John Jacobs, "Thomas Mofolo en de Negro-Afrikaanse literatuur," *Vlaamse Gids*, XLVII (1963), 199–206; Daniel P. Kunene and Randal A. Kirsch, *The Beginning of South African Vernacular Literature*, n.p., n.d. [Los Angeles, 1967], pp. 43–46.

3. Apart from the Bible, Bunyan's work is the most widely translated book in the vernacular languages of Africa. The Sotho version was due to the Rev. Mabille and printed at Morija in 1872; it reached its seventh printing in 1945.

4. M. M. Mahood, "Marie Corelli in West Africa," *Ibadan*, V (February 1959), 19–21. Miss Mahood gives the following main reasons for this writer's odd popularity in Africa: hers were among the first works available to Africans with a reading knowledge of English; she takes a strong stand against secular education and the "new woman"; her exuberant prose and her zest for the supernatural.

5. *Livre d'or des missions du Lessouto* (Paris: Société des Missions Evangéliques), p. 508. This novel was translated as *The Traveller of the East* (London: S.P.C.K., 1934); part of it was also translated into French; "Géorgiques et voyages du chrétien au Lessouto. Fekesi," *Le Monde non-chrétien*, n.s. No. 11 (1949), 349–58. See Alice Werner, "A Mosuto Novelist," *International Review of Missions*, XIV (1925), 428–36, and G. A. Gollock, "*The Traveller of the East*, by Thomas Mofolo," *Africa*, VII (1934), 510–11. The most convenient general survey of Mofolo's writings is Daniel P. Kunene, *The Works of Thomas Mofolo. Summaries and Critiques*, Los Angeles, University of California African Studies Center Occasional Paper No. 2 (1967).

6. The correct English spelling is Shaka, although Tshaka can also be found. I shall use Mofolo's spelling, which was taught him by the French missionaries.

7. Subtitles of the English version by F. H. Dutton (London, 1931), which also has a very perceptive introduction by Sir Henry Newbolt.

8. Subtitle of the French translation by V. Ellenberger (Paris, 1940).

9. *Chaka*, p. 13. Page references are to the English edition. The German critic Janheinz Jahn informs me that a few pages of the original Sotho text have not been translated by Dutton. As the English edition is out of print, a new, revised edition is certainly called for.

10. Kunene, *The Works of Thomas Mofolo*, p. 26.

11. Ezekiel Mphahlele, *The African Image*, (London, 1962), p. 171.

12. *Journal of the African Society*, XXX (1931), 38.

13. *South African Outlook*, LXII (1932), 19.

14. M. L[eenhardt], "Chaka, Fidélité et infidélité chez les paiens," *Le Monde non-chrétien*, I (1947), 346–48.

15. Luc Decaunes, "Une épopée bantoue," *Présence Africaine*, No. 5 (1948), 883–86. See also on *Chaka*: Edwin W. Smith's review in *Africa*, IV (1931), 506–8; John Jacobs, "Les

épopées de Soundjata et de Chaka: une étude comparée," *Aequatoria*, XXV (1962), 121–24; O. R. Dathorne, "Thomas Mofolo and the Sotho Hero," *New African*, V (1966), 152–53.

16. P.–D. Beuchat, *Do the Bantu Have a Literature?* (Johannesburg, n.d. [1963]), p. 19.

17. L. B. Saratoyskaya, "Periodizatsia literary Bantu y Yuzhno-Afrikanstrom Souze (nachaliniy period)," *Narodi Azii i Afriki*, I (1963), 117–27. This critic also regresses beyond even Alice Werner and D. D. T. Jabavu, claiming that Mofolo was subjected to the influence of the official South African historians who were bent on reviling the Zulus' heroic struggle against colonialism, so that he represented Chaka as a "beastly power-drunk creature."

18. Mphahlele, *African Image*, p. 172.

19. Claude Wauthier, *The Literature and Thought of Modern Africa* (New York, 1966), p. 96.

20. Kunene, *The Works of Thomas Mofolo*, p. 26.

21. This is the theme of *Song of a Goat*, a play by Nigeria's John Pepper Clark. Such attitudes are of course not restricted to African societies: it would be interesting to compare what Mofolo has to say and Clark's tragedy with Federico Garçia Lorca's *Yerma*.

22. According to recent historians, Chaka was actually impotent.

23. Janheinz Jahn, *Geschichte der neoafrikanischen Literatur* (Düsseldorf, 1966), p. 108.

24. I am gratefully indebted to the Rev. Albert Brutsch for the information in the next two paragraphs.

25. Jahn, p. 108, also mentions an Italian translation, without providing any bibliographical data. It may be added that an abridged version of the French translation was published in the Congo-Kinshasa: Leverville, Bibliothèque de l'Etoile, 1958.

26. Kunene and Kirsch, *The Beginning of South African Vernacular Literature*, p. 8.

27. We may recall at this point that in 1636 Richelieu obliged Corneille to delete a few lines from *Le Cid* because they seemed to glorify the illegal custom of the duel; actually they were spoken in character, and the apology they contained is denied by the total context of the play. Richelieu, however, was not concerned with aesthetics but with consolidating absolute monarchy, and he feared—no doubt rightly from his political viewpoint—the electrifying effect which such lines, taken out of

context, might have on a seventeenth-century aristocratic audience.

Demonic Strategies: *The Birthday Party* and *The Firebugs*
HEILMAN

1. Quotations are from Harold Pinter, *The Birthday Party*, Methuen's Modern Plays (London, 1963).

2. Quotations are from Max Frisch, *The Firebugs*, tr. Mordecai Gorelik, A Spotlight Dramabook (New York, 1963). This version, including the Epilogue, may be found in *Masters of Modern Drama*, ed. Haskell M. Bloch and Robert G. Shedd (New York, 1962).

3. Cf. Martin Esslin, *The Theatre of the Absurd*, Anchor Books (Garden City, 1961), p. 193.

4. Esslin names this as one of a number of possible interpretations, but his view is that any interpretation, especially of an "over-all allegorical" kind, too much restricts the significance of the play (*The Theatre of the Absurd*, pp. 204–5). Nevertheless, reading Stanley as artist conforms to numerous details of action and symbol. Obviously it is not the only way to approach an ambiguous play, but there is much evidence to make it convincing. Walter Kerr is sure that Pinter's work is all existence and no essence; there is only "blind collision," and no "Platonic" ideas are implied by undefined characters. See Walter Kerr, *Harold Pinter*, Columbia Essays on Modern Writers (New York and London, 1967), especially pp. 22–25. But it is possible that Pinter, though he says "I don't conceptualize in any way" (Kerr, p. 9), may, through the natural action of the human imagination, fall into some Platonizing after all.

The Upward Path: Notes on the Work of Katherine Anne Porter BAKER

1. This essay, revised for this book, appeared earlier in the *Southern Review*, n.s. (Winter 1968), 1–19.

2. Reprinted in *The Collected Stories of Katherine Anne Porter* (New York, 1965). This collection will be the source of my references to Miss Porter's stories, unless I indicate otherwise.

3. George Hendrick, *Katherine Anne Porter* (New York, 1965); William L. Nance, *Katherine Anne Porter* (New York, 1965).

4. Katherine Anne Porter, *The Days Before* (New York, 1952). This collection will be the source of my references to Miss Porter's prose, unless I indicate otherwise.

The Way to Read *Gatsby* FOSTER

1. In *The Modern Novel in America* (rev. ed.; Chicago, 1963), p. 91, Frederick J. Hoffman writes that Ford's successful use of the " 'qualified first-person' narrator" in *The Good Soldier* "had an effect upon F. Scott Fitzgerald which can be seen in his use of Nick Carraway in *The Great Gatsby*," though he cites no evidence for the influence and elsewhere (see below) seems unwilling to accept the kind of reading of *Gatsby* that might issue from the assumption of such an influence if it could be established.

The three commentaries alluded to above are as follows: Robert W. Stallman, "Gatsby and the Hole in Time," in *The House that James Built* (East Lansing, 1961); Frederick J. Hoffman, *"The Great Gatsby": A Study* (New York, 1962), p. 337; Gary J. Scrimgeour, "Against The Great Gatsby," *Criticism*, VIII (Winter 1966), 75–86.

Mark Twain Among the Malefactors LEARY

1. Some part of this essay was delivered as a lecture in January, 1968, before the Friends of the University of Miami Library, and some part of that was published in June, 1968, in their journal, *The Carrell*. The friendship between these two men is detailed in my edition of *Mark Twain's Correspondence with Henry Huttleston Rogers, 1893–1909*, published in 1969 by the University of California Press as a volume in the Mark Twain Papers.

The Pisan Cantos: The Form of Survival SUTTON

1. The text followed here is that of *The Cantos of Ezra Pound, 1–95* (New York, 1965). Individual cantos are cited in parentheses in Arabic numerals, regardless of the numeral form observed in Pound's text.

Index